Nicolae Sfetcu

# ADVANCED PERSISTENT THREATS
# in CYBERSECURITY
## CYBER WARFARE

MultiMedia

Bucharest, 2024

DOI: 10.58679/MM28378

MultiMedia
Bucharest, 2024
Email: office@multimedia.com.ro

# CONTENTS

# ABSTRACT

This book aims to provide a comprehensive analysis of Advanced Persistent Threats (APTs), including their characteristics, origins, methods, consequences, and defense strategies, with a focus on detecting these threats. It explores the concept of advanced persistent threats in the context of cyber security and cyber warfare. APTs represent one of the most insidious and challenging forms of cyber threats, characterized by their sophistication, persistence, and targeted nature. The paper examines the origins, characteristics and methods used by APT actors. It also explores the complexities associated with APT detection, analyzing the evolving tactics used by threat actors and the corresponding advances in detection methodologies. It highlights the importance of a multi-faceted approach that integrates technological innovations with proactive defense strategies to effectively identify and mitigate APT.

**Keywords**: Advanced Persistent Threats, APT, cybersecurity. cyber warfare, threat detection, cyberattack

# 1 INTRODUCTION

This book aims to provide a comprehensive analysis of Advanced Persistent Threats (APTs), including their characteristics, origins, methods, consequences, and defense strategies, with a focus on detecting these threats. He explores the concept of advanced persistent threats in the context of cyber security and cyber warfare. APTs represent one of the most insidious and challenging forms of cyber threats, characterized by their sophistication, persistence, and targeted nature. The paper discusses the potential consequences of APT attacks, as well as strategies and best practices for defending against them. In addition, it highlights the importance of international cooperation in the fight against APT and provides insights into the evolving cybersecurity landscape in the face of this ongoing threat.

# CYBERSECURITY

Cyber security is the totality of measures to protect computer systems and networks against attacks by malicious actors that can affect digital or physical assets, or the image of a person or organization, disrupt a certain activity or negatively influence a certain trend (Schatz, Bashroush, and Wall 2017).

The field of cyber security is in constant flux, adapting to the ever-changing digital landscape. As technology advances, so do the tactics of cybercriminals.

Cybersecurity has become an integral part of modern society, with the digital revolution significantly affecting our daily lives, and is one of the most important challenges of the contemporary world, due to both the complexity of information systems and today's society. As we increasingly rely on interconnected systems, the need to protect our data and infrastructure from cyber threats becomes paramount (Stevens 2018).

Cybersecurity is an ever-evolving field that requires constant adaptation to new challenges. To meet these challenges, advanced threat detection, user education and international cooperation are key components of an effective cyber security strategy.

# Challenges in cyber security

Rapid technological advances
- The constant evolution of technology leads to new vulnerabilities.
- Cybercriminals exploit emerging technologies for malicious purposes.
- Keeping up with security measures becomes a daunting task.

Diversity of cyber threats (CloudStrike 2023)
- The range of cyber threats, including malware, ransomware, phishing, and others, pose significant challenges.
- Sophisticated attack techniques are continuously evolving, making detection and prevention difficult.

Human error and insider threats (Lim et al. 2009)
- People often remain the weakest link in cyber security.
- Insider threats, whether intentional or unintentional, can be devastating.

Resource limitations
- Limited budgets and resources prevent comprehensive cybersecurity efforts.
- Smaller organizations are particularly vulnerable to these constraints.

International and geopolitical challenges
- Cyberspace knows no borders, leading to international and geopolitical conflicts in the digital realm.
- International cooperation and cyber diplomacy are essential.

# Solutions in cyber security

Advanced threat detection
- Using artificial intelligence and machine learning for real-time threat detection.
- Developing proactive threat intelligence mechanisms to anticipate attacks.

User education and awareness (Townsend 2018)
- Training employees to recognize and respond to cyber threats.
- Promoting a culture of cyber security in organizations.

Multi-Factor Authentication (MFA)
- Using MFA to improve user authentication.
- Reducing the impact of stolen or weak passwords.

Cyber Security Regulations and Compliance (Shirey 2000)
- Develop and enforce regulations to hold organizations accountable for cybersecurity issues.
- Mandatory data protection measures and incident reporting.

International cooperation
- Promoting international collaboration in addressing cyber threats.
- Developing cyber norms and agreements to reduce conflicts in cyberspace.
-

# CYBER WARFARE

Cyber warfare involves the use of cyberattacks at the state level, causing damage comparable to real warfare and/or disrupting enemy infrastructure and systems (Singer and Friedman 2014).

Taddeo offered the following definition of cyber warfare in 2012:

"Warfare based on certain uses of ICT within an offensive or defensive military strategy supported by a state and aimed at the disruption or immediate control of enemy resources and conducted in the information environment, with agents and targets varying both physically. and non-physical domains and whose level of violence may vary according to circumstances." (Taddeo 2012)

Cybersecurity and cyber warfare have become critical issues. Cybersecurity (the practice of safeguarding digital systems and data from malicious activity) is inextricably linked to cyberwarfare, which involves the use of digital technologies to disrupt, damage, or gain control over adversary computer systems. The line between these two areas is blurred, as cybersecurity strategies often have dual use as applications in cyber warfare and vice versa.

Cybersecurity and cyber warfare are intertwined in a complex relationship that shapes our digital world. As cyber threats continue to evolve, and nation-states engage in offensive cyber actions, the need for robust cybersecurity measures and international cooperation is more critical than ever. To effectively navigate this complicated nexus, stakeholders must continually adapt to the dynamic nature of the cyber domain, recognizing that digital warfare is as important as any physical battlefield in the 21st century.

The threat landscape is constantly evolving, requiring adaptive cybersecurity measures. Cyber threats encompass a wide range of activities, including data theft, malware attacks, denial-of-service attacks, and social engineering. These threats can target individuals, organizations, or even entire nations. As cyber threats grow in complexity, so does the challenge of securing critical infrastructure and sensitive information.

## Challenges in maintaining cybersecurity

More than 120 countries have developed ways to use cyber warfare as a weapon and target financial markets, government IT systems and utilities. It can be used to support traditional warfare, or for espionage and propaganda purposes. Cyber weapons have the potential to be as destructive as traditional ones (Shamah, n.d.).

**Advanced Persistent Threats (APTs)**: APTs are sophisticated, long-term cyberattacks, often led by nation states or well-funded groups. Detecting and mitigating APTs is a significant challenge because they use advanced tactics to evade traditional security measures.

**Human factors**: Human error, negligence, or insider threats can undermine cybersecurity. Addressing these issues requires not only technical solutions but also organizational culture and awareness.

**Rapid technological advances**: As technology advances, new vulnerabilities emerge. There is a need to keep pace with the ever-changing threat landscape through continuous innovation in cybersecurity practices.

## Implications of cyber warfare

**Geopolitical impact**: Nation-states are engaging in cyber warfare to achieve strategic objectives without resorting to traditional military action. Examples include Stuxnet, a computer worm designed to disrupt Iran's nuclear program, and alleged Russian meddling in foreign elections. Such actions can destabilize international relations.

**Role of non-state actors**: Non-state actors, such as hacktivists and cyber criminals, play a significant role in cyber warfare. They can be hired or influenced by nation-states to carry out attacks, blurring the lines between independent and state-sponsored cyber warfare.

**Escalation dilemma**: The anonymity and deniability associated with cyberattacks raises concerns about the potential for unintended escalation in conflict. A minor cyber incident can inadvertently lead to a large-scale conflict.

In an increasingly interconnected global situation, international cooperation is imperative in addressing the challenges of cybersecurity and cyber warfare. Establishing norms and regulations can help mitigate the risks associated with state sponsorship and cyber warfare, promote responsible behavior in cyberspace, and provide a framework for responding to cyber incidents.

Currently, many analysts believe that the sure solution to state cyber threats is a cyber peace through political decision, establishing new rules and international norms and building new tools and infrastructures suitable for this purpose. (Hofkirchner and Burgin 2017).

The future of cyber security and cyber warfare remains uncertain. Emerging technologies such as quantum computing and artificial intelligence are expected to revolutionize both offensive and defensive capabilities. As such, the global community must anticipate the evolving threat landscape and adapt its strategies accordingly.

# 2 ADVANCED PERSISTENT THREATS

Advanced persistent threats (APTs) are a class of cyber threats that pose a significant challenge to organizations and nations around the world. They are known for their advanced tactics, techniques, and procedures, as well as their ability to infiltrate and operate persistently on target systems for long periods of time.

APTs are usually coordinated by a state or a state-sponsored group (Kaspersky 2023b) (Cisco 2023). The motivations of these threat actors are usually military, geopolitical, or economic espionage (Cole 2013). These targeted sectors include government, defense, financial services, legal services, industrial, telecommunications, consumer goods, and more (FireEye 2019).

The average "contact time," in which an APT attack goes undetected, averaged 71 days in North America, 177 days in EMEA, and 204 days in APAC in 2018 (Mandiant 2021).

Advanced persistent threats combine a variety of different forms of attack, from social engineering to technical exploits. APTs generally use traditional espionage vectors (Ghafir and Prenosil 2014), including social engineering, human intelligence, and infiltration, for network attacks by installing custom malware (malicious software) (Symantec 2018b). The diversity and stealth of APTs make them a central issue in cyber security due to the asymmetric nature of attacks, often turning to game theory to model conflict using matrix games as a risk mitigation tool. Game-theoretic APT models can be derived directly from topological vulnerability analysis, together with risk assessments, according to common risk management standards such as the ISO 31000 family (Rass, König, and Schauer 2017)

Increasing heterogeneity, connectivity and openness of information systems allow access to a system through multiple different paths. To ensure security, semi-automated tools and techniques are used to detect and mitigate vulnerabilities, but such attacks quickly adapt to these configurations so that they stay "under the radar". Countermeasures have a higher latency, being ineffective for sudden changes in attack strategies of an invisible adversary (Rass, König, and Schauer 2017).

Advanced persistent threats have emerged as a new and complex version of multi-stage attacks (MSA) (Kyriakopoulos et al. 2018), while current APT detection systems focus more on the emergence of alerts of detection, than on predicting threats (Ghafir et al. 2019). APT stage forecasting not only reveals the APT lifecycle in its early stages, but also helps in understanding the attacker's strategies and objectives. In addition, the Internet of Things (IoT) makes Internet-connected devices easy targets for cyberattacks (Ghafir, Kyriakopoulos, et al. 2018). The global cost of cybercrime reached $600 billion in 2018, according to a McAfee report (McAfee 2018).

To counter cyberattacks, analysts typically use Intrusion Detection Systems (IDS) by matching known (signature-based) attack patterns by comparing the data to a database containing a list of known attack signatures), or observing anomalies (deviation from a reference profile) (Santoro et al. 2017). The targeted objective of APT is espionage and data exfiltration. The attack can last for weeks or years, with very long periods between the stages of the attack. making it difficult to detect by correlating multiple alerts during the APT lifecycle (Mandiant 2013). Traditional pattern matching methods are ineffective in the case of APT, as there is no pattern of order and frequencies between stages, due to technical limitations of the static mechanisms of the attacked institution or the attacker's use of new and dynamic techniques. An APT unfolds in several stages, with the attacker's privileges, information, and resources accumulating at each stage.

In 76% of organizations affected by APTs, antivirus software and threat detection systems were ineffective. At the Infosecurity Europe 2011 conference, APTs were included among the biggest cyber threats of the modern world (Rot and Olszewski 2017). According to a Deloitte report (Deloitte 2016), the key factors in combating APT are: constant risk assessment, offensive security, and staff training (Rot 2009).

# Definition of APT

A common cyberattack aims to exploit vulnerabilities to steal data from companies (P. Chen, Desmet, and Huygens 2014), causing non-critical damage. An APT has far more resources and focuses on large organizations and government institutions, causing serious, even critical, damage.

Many feel that the term APT is overloaded because different people refer to it as different things. The definition given by the US National Institute of Standards and Technology (NIST) states that an APT is (NIST 2011):

"An adversary that possesses sophisticated levels of expertise and significant resources which allow it to create opportunities to achieve its objectives by using multiple attack vectors (e.g., cyber, physical, and deception). These objectives typically include establishing and extending footholds within the information technology infrastructure of the targeted organizations for purposes of exfiltrating information, undermining or impeding critical aspects of a mission, program, or organization; or positioning itself to carry out these objectives in the future. The advanced persistent threat: (i) pursues its objectives repeatedly over an extended period of time; (ii) adapts to defenders' efforts to resist it; and (iii) is determined to maintain the level of interaction needed to execute its objectives."

The main features of an APT follow from its name itself:

- **Threat** – APTs have both capability and intent, being executed through coordinated actions, with qualified, motivated, organized and well-funded personnel (Maloney 2018) (IT Governance 2023).
- **Persistence** – Attackers use a "low and slow" approach within a coherent strategy; if they lose access to their target, they will try again to get it. Their goals are to maintain long-term access (IT Governance 2023) (Arntz 2016).
- **Advanced** – Attackers have a wide range of state-of-the-art techniques and tools, some even innovative, and may include commonly available components. They typically attempt to establish multiple entry points into targeted networks, and combine multiple methods, tools, and techniques to achieve their goals, maintain access, and compromise the target (Maloney 2018) (Arntz 2016).

The specificity of APTs allows them to retain access even if malicious activity is discovered and an incident response is triggered allowing cybersecurity defenders to close a compromise.

## History of APT

Attacks on cybersecurity via targeted email combined with social engineering and using trojans to exfiltrate information have been used as far back as the early 1990s, being made known by UK and US CERTs in 2005. The term "advanced persistent threat" was first used in the United States Air Force in 2006 (SANS 2013), by Colonel Greg Rattray (Holland 2013).

Through the Stuxnet project, the US targeted the computer hardware of Iran's nuclear program, an example of an APT attack (Virvilis and Gritzalis 2013).

PC World reported an 81% increase in APTs from 2010 to 2011. Several countries have used cyberspace to collect information through APTs (Grow, Epstein, and Tschang 2008), through affiliated groups or agents of sovereign state governments (Daly 2009).

A Bell Canada study found widespread APT presence in Canadian government and critical infrastructure, with attacks attributed to Chinese and Russian actors (McMahon and Rohozinski 2013).

Google, Adobe Systems, Juniper Networks and Symantec were victims of an APT attack called Operation Aurora (Matthews 2019).

Several attacks in the military, financial, energy, nuclear, education, aerospace, telecommunications, chemical, and government sectors were reported in 2011 (Y. Wang et al. 2016). The most publicized APT attacks include Stuxnet, RAS Breach, Operation Aurora, Duqu, Operation Ke3chang, Flame, Snow Man, Red October and Mini duke, with more recent malware attacks Ratankba, ActiveX, etc. (Xu et al. 2015). Their usual objectives are cyber espionage with national security interests and sabotage of strategic infrastructures. Attacks use hardware devices and software tools, with a systematic approach that often relies on social engineering as the main mechanism to gain access and zero-day exploits (Adelaiye, Ajibola, and Silas 2019).

Industroyer, a malware framework that was discovered in 2016, targeted the power grid in the capital of Ukraine, causing a short-term power outage in that area (Tollefson 2020).

# FEATURES OF APT

Advanced persistent threats are characterized by persistence (remaining undetected in a target environment for long periods, sometimes even years), pinpoint targeting (selective, tailoring their attacks to the vulnerabilities or weaknesses of targets), and sophistication (advanced and cutting-edge techniques generation, some even innovative, often using zero-day exploits, social engineering, and other sophisticated methods).

The distinctive characteristics of APT are (P. Chen, Desmet, and Huygens 2014):

**Specific targets and clear objectives**. The targets of APT attacks are specific, usually governments, organizations, or countries' militaries, limiting their attack range. Their purpose is mostly strategic benefits in national security and obtaining secret information.

**Expert, organized and resourceful attackers**. Attackers are usually skilled hackers working in a coordinated manner, employed in a government/military cyber unit (Mandiant 2013) or cyber mercenaries, prepared to operate for extended periods of time and exploit zero-day vulnerabilities. Sometimes they can even operate with the support of military or state intelligence services.

**Long-term attacks and, if necessary, repeated attempts**. APT campaigns go undetected for months or years. APT actors are constantly adapting their efforts to changing conditions or to overcome a particular difficulty.

**Stealth and evasive techniques**. APT attacks can remain undetected, hiding in network traffic and interacting minimally, only to achieve defined objectives. They can use zero-day exploits to avoid signature-based detection, and encryption to spoof network traffic.

|  | Traditional Attacks | APT Attacks |
|---|---|---|
| Attacker | Mostly single person | Highly organized, sophisticated, determined, and well-resourced group |
| Target | Unspecified, mostly individual systems | Specific organizations, governmental institutions, commercial enterprises |
| Purpose | Financial benefits, demonstrating abilities | Competitive advantages, strategic benefits |
| Approach | Single run, "smash and grab", short period | Repeated attempts, stays low and slow, adapts to resist defenses, long term |

Table 1: Comparison of traditional and APT attacks. Source (P. Chen, Desmet, and Huygens 2014)

# APT METHODS, TECHNIQUES, AND MODELS

APTs use a variety of methods and techniques, the most used being (Quintero-Bonilla and Martín del Rey 2020):

1.  *Phishing and spear-phishing* (targeted email phishing): APT actors often initiate their attacks through deceptive email campaigns, tricking employees into clicking on malicious links or downloading infected attachments (Aleroud and Zhou 2017).
2.  *Social engineering*: Determining a user with specific permissions on the network to act in a way that will compromise information systems (Krombholz et al. 2015).
3.  *Unintentional download (drive-by-download)*: It causes the unintended download and execution (without users'

knowledge) of malicious software from the Internet (Tanaka, Akiyama, and Goto 2017), using for this purpose integrated plugins such as ActiveX, Java/JavaScript or Adobe Flash player (Nick 2018).

4. *Zero-day exploit* (vulnerabilities unknown to victims): APTs frequently exploit undisclosed (zero-day) vulnerabilities in software and hardware to gain unauthorized access.

5. *Malware and backdoors*: APTs use sophisticated malware and backdoors to maintain a persistent presence in compromised systems, enabling data exfiltration and continuous control.

6. *Watering hole*: The attack is similar to spear-phishing, adapted to the needs of the victims (Fortinet 2023).

**Social engineering** is a primary tool in the initial stages of APT (Adelaiye, Ajibola, and Silas 2019). In general, "social engineering attacks are security exploits that prey on the vulnerable attributes of humans rather than of technology" (Parrish, Jr, Bailey, and Courtney 2009). SRI International defines social engineering as deceptive practices to obtain information from people using social, business or technical discourse (S. Cobb 1996). The social engineering taxonomy presented by Krombholz et al. (Krombholz et al. 2015) suggests four crucial aspects to consider in social engineering attacks: channel, type, operator, and attack vectors. Email, instant messaging, Skype, Dropbox, LinkedIn, Lync, etc. are usually used as attack vectors. According to Radha Gulati (Gulati 2003), social engineering targets certain attributes of human behavior, such as trust, the desire to be helpful, the desire to get something for nothing, curiosity, fear of the unknown or of losing something (like when responding to pop-up windows), ignorance and carelessness (Bere et al. 2015). Trash searches are part of social engineering, being used to create personalized profiles of victims. Reverse social engineering (Mitnick and Simon 2011) uses sabotage, advertising, and assistance to gain access to desired information, for example through a USB drive that may contain a Trojan horse (Krombholz et al. 2015). Another common attack considered to be part of social engineering is click jacking, also known as "Ul-redressing" (Chaitanya et al. 2012), whereby users arrive in dangerous areas thinking they have clicked a legitimate button.

In APTs, it is difficult to identify who the attacker is, as they often use the concept of false flag, impersonating someone else, to camouflage their operations. The main countries from which these attacks originate, which are carried out in carefully planned campaigns with customized methods and techniques, are (Quintero-Bonilla and Martín del Rey 2020):

- *China*: Attacks focused on industrial espionage. APT1 was the most persistent cyber threat from this actor (Mandiant 2013).

- *United States of America*: Conducted the most sophisticated cyberattacks, especially to enforce its geopolitical interests. A classic example is the Stuxnet operation (Falliere, Murchu, and Chien 2011), which targeted SCADA (Supervisory Control and Data Acquisition) systems to delay Iran's nuclear program.
- *Russia*: Many state-sponsored attacks (Lemay et al. 2018). APT28 spear-phishing attacks detected by Microsoft, targeting German government employees (ETDA 2023).
- *Iran*: Identified as the Middle East actor with the most attacks (Lemay et al. 2018), such as APT33 operations. The attacks targeted large industrial targets, but also organizations in the United States, the Middle East and Asia (Paganini 2019).
- *North Korea*: Numerous espionage, financial and destructive attacks, such as the WannaCry ransomware (Adams 2018).
- *Israel*: Possible co-author of the Stuxnet attack (Falliere, Murchu, and Chien 2011). Unit 8200(CSS 2019) of the Israeli army, the equivalent of the American intelligence agency NSA, is one of the agencies particularly competent in APTs, such as the Duqu 2.0 attack (Kaspersky 2015) which has infected numerous systems in several countries in recent years using zero-day vulnerabilities.

In addition to state actors, there are privately funded and non-governmental cybercriminal groups using various methods of propagation. In general, the cyber espionage carried out by these actors targets diplomatic organizations and the information technology industry (Kaspersky 2023a).

According to the EC-Council, " Threat modeling can be defined as a structured processing which IT professionals and cybersecurity experts can detect likely security vulnerabilities and threats, measure the severity of each potential impact, and prioritize methods to protect IT infrastructure and mitigate attacks" (EC-Council 2023) (H. Hejase, Kazan, and Moukadem 2020). In addition, threat modeling methodologies can be applied to develop:

1. A collection of probable threats that may occur.
2. An abstraction of the system.
3. Profiles of likely malicious attackers, their objectives and techniques (EC-Council 2023).

According to Microsoft, "threat modeling is a core element of the Microsoft Security Development Lifecycle (SDL). It's an engineering technique one can use to help identify threats, attacks, vulnerabilities, and countermeasures that could affect one's application. Threat modeling is used to shape one's application's design, meet the company's security objectives, and reduce risk." (Microsoft 2022) (H. Hejase, Kazan, and Moukadem 2020).

There are five major steps of threat modeling: defining security requirements; creating an application diagram; identifying threats; mitigating threats; and validating that threats have been mitigated. (H. Hejase, Kazan, and Moukadem 2020)

Microsoft says the "threat modeling tool" allows any developer or software architect to:

1. Communicates the security design of their systems.
2. Analyze c-models for potential security issues using a proven methodology.
3. Suggest and manage security mitigation measures (Microsoft 2022) (H. Hejase, Kazan, and Moukadem 2020).

The PASTA model (Z. Chen et al. 2022) considers seven stages, which include business goal definition, technical domain definition, application decomposition, threat analysis, vulnerability detection, attack enumeration, and impact analysis (Shevchenko et al. 2018).

# APT life cycle

Several variants have been studied for APT life cycles, with different stages but similar methods and techniques (Quintero-Bonilla and Martín del Rey 2020). Each stage in the life cycle can in turn be divided into several sub-stages to deepen the understanding of the operation of APT. Each stage is characterized by specific tactics, techniques, and procedures (TTP). The first steps are generally to study and analyze the target. An exploit then takes place, followed by discreet data mining on a command and control (C&C) server. The Mandiant lifecycle describes cleanup as a final step, to avoid detection of the attack. Each attacker can plan stages in any order and use tailored TTPs to accomplish objectives.

### ATP in three stages

Ussath et al. al. (Ussath et al. 2016) discussed a 3-stage APT attack lifecycle model that focuses only on the representative characteristics of an attack, based on the analysis of different methods and techniques of 22 APT campaigns:

1. *Initial compromise*: Attackers try to access the target system. Techniques used: spear-phishing, watering-hole, attacks on the server exploiting its vulnerabilities or brute force, and infected storage media (USB, CD, DVD).

2. *Lateral movement*: Compromising other collateral services in the system or network using obtained credentials. Techniques used: RDP, PsExec, Powershell, and exploiting vulnerabilities through, e.g., zero-day exploitation.
3. *Command and control*: Establishing an external connection to exfiltrate data. Services used: HTTP, HTTPS or FTP, and remote connection techniques such as VNC (Virtual Network Computing) or RDP.

In the case of IoT networks, APT attacks are difficult to counter due to the combination of several techniques (Sriram et al. 2020). *APT botnet* is one of the most critical attacks in IoT networks, using malware to take control of equipment connected to web services. The botnet is controlled by the botmaster, the main computer capable of injecting large-scale activity (Waqas et al. 2022). The life cycle of a botnet attack can consist of spread/injection, control, and enforcement (Hachem et al. 2011).

## ATP in four stages

The *intrusion kill chain (IKC)* is a model that identifies the behaviors and goals of an APT attack (R. Zhang et al. 2017), in four stages (Quintero-Bonilla and Martín del Rey 2020):
1. *Collection of information*: With scanning tools or through social engineering.
2. *Intrusion*: Using spear-phishing or backdoor techniques to gain access.
3. *Latent expansion*: Maintaining control and network expansion.
4. *Information theft*: Establishing an external connection for data transfer, possibly using encryption techniques to disguise the extracted data.

Wang et al. (Xu Wang et al. 2016) propose another four-stage life cycle approach:
1. *Initial compromise*: The techniques used are social engineering and spear-phishing.
2. *Command and control*: Creating a communication channel between a server and the target.
3. *Lateral movement*: Gathering information, moving between hosts with vulnerabilities.
4. *Attack*: Complete, information theft begins.

## ATP in five stages

Sexton, Storlie, and Neil (Sexton, Storlie, and Neil 2015) propose a five-stage model; called *kill chain*:

1. *Delivery*: Spear-phishing is used through malicious messages.
2. *Exploit*: Exploitation of vulnerabilities.
3. *Installation*: Malware, such as RATs (remote access tools).
4. *Command and control*: Remote access to the compromised target.
5. *Actions*: Using access to extract information.

Jeun, Lee, and Won (Jeun, Lee, and Won 2012) describe another five-stage model:

1. *Recount*: Select the target and obtain the necessary attack information.
2. *Intrusion*: Gaining access through stolen credentials with techniques such as SQL injection or malware.
3. *Discovery*: The target system is searched for confidential data.
4. *Capture*: Installing a rootkit to collect data over an extended period.
5. *Exfiltration*: Collected data is sent to command-and-control servers.

Alshamrani et al. (Alshamrani et al. 2019) consider that the 5-stage APT could represent every APT attack, regardless of the objective, while showing how the objective can change the stages involved:

1. *Reconnaissance*: Marks the beginning of any attack, to know the target.
2. *Foothold establishment*: Represents the attackers' successful entry into the target's computer and/or network. by exploiting vulnerabilities, malware, spear phishing, zero-day exploit, web download and phishing attacks.
3. *Lateral movement*: Attackers should move laterally in the target's network to search for other components or data.
4. *Exfiltration/damage*: Retrieving and sending data to the command and control center, or disabling or destroying critical components of the target organization.
5. *Post-exfiltration/post-damage*: Continue exfiltration or disable other important components or delete evidence for a clean exit.

The first 2 stages are required for success. The other 3 stages are applicable depending on the attacker's objective.

## APT in six stages

Ghafir and Prenosil (Ghafir and Prenosil 2016) proposed a model where attackers have to trick a person into running malware and exploit any zero-day vulnerability:

1. *Information gathering*: Information about the target's structure through public social network profiles.
2. *Entry point*: Using social engineering, spear-phishing and zero-day exploits to gain access.
3. *Command and control server*: A connection is established between the compromised host and the C&C server, using Secure Sockets Layer (SSL) encryption to send traffic to the server.
4. *Lateral movement*: Moving through the network to find other vulnerable hosts.
5. *Data*: Identify critical information of interest.
6. *External server*: Data is transmitted to C&C servers.

Ping Chen, Lieven Desmet, and Christophe Huygens adopted a lifecycle model of the intrusion destruction chain (P. Chen, Desmet, and Huygens 2014):

1. *Reconnaissance and staffing*: The study and collection of technical information about the target and key personnel, using techniques such as social engineering, and gathering information from publicly available sources (OSINT) by aggregating information about an employee's personal profile or hardware configurations and software in an organization. An attack plan is developed, and the necessary tools are prepared, for different attack vectors for flexibility of tactics.
2. *Delivery*: Delivering exploits to targets, directly (e.g. through social engineering - spear-phishing, with drive-by-download exploits or watering hole techniques (Trend 2012)) or indirectly (covertly) by compromising and using the resources of a third party (such as a software/hardware vendor).
3. *Initial intrusion*: With the help of obtained credentials the target is accessed, and malicious code is executed exploiting the vulnerabilities. Access credentials can be obtained through social engineering or the execution of delivered malicious code that exploits a vulnerability. Attackers often exploit vulnerabilities in Adobe PDF, Adobe Flash, Microsoft Office, and Internet Explorer. Although it is preferable to use zero-day

exploits at this stage (McAfee 2010a), older exploits can also be used for non-updated installed applications. After the backdoor malware is installed, the connection to the target is made, generating network traffic recorded in the logs, with the risk of possible detection.

4. *Command and control*: A mechanism is established to take control of compromised targets; avoiding detection by posting to social networking sites (IC Espionage 2010), TOR anonymity networks, or using remote access tools (RATs) (Villeneuve and Bennett 2014).

5. *Lateral movement*: Moving in the network for useful information to the intended purpose and to gain access to other systems as well, through activities such as internal reconnaissance to map the network and obtain information; collecting credentials by compromising additional systems and identifying and collecting data of interest. This stage is much larger than the others in order to maximize the volume of information by running at an undetectably low and slow pace.

6. *Exfiltration of data*: Transmission of encrypted information to servers. Exfiltration is a critical step for attackers, where data is compressed and often encrypted internally for transmission to external locations, often using secure protocols such as SSL/TLS, or the anonymity feature of the Tor network (IC Espionage 2010).

In the mathematical framework of the relevant algorithms used by the proposed prediction system (Markov chain, hidden Markov model, Viterbi algorithm and Baum-Welch algorithm), Ghafir et al. highlight the following life cycle of APT (Ghafir et al. 2019):

1. Information gathering: Information is obtained about the target organization (structure, IT environment, employees, etc.), using public sources (social networks, web pages, etc.) and social engineering. The information allows the creation of spear phishing emails.

2. *Initial compromise (Point of Entry)*: By using social engineering and spear phishing or by exploiting software vulnerabilities, or by installing malware on a website visited by the victim's employees.

3. *Command and Control (C&C) communication*: Communication between the infected host and the C&C server for commands, usually protected by Secure Sockets Layer (SSL), or/and using the domain flow technique (Yadav et al. 2012) by which a exploited host may try to connect to a large number of domain names, all of which are fake except the C&C server, making it difficult or even impossible to shut down all of these domain names.

4. *Lateral movement*: Moving laterally through the target's network for new hosts to infect, using brute force or legitimate access data. Another technique is the hash attack, using an encrypted authentication by the victim to trick the authentication system into creating a new session on the same network (J. Johnson and Hogan 2013).

5. *Asset identification*: Finding data of interest for the exfiltration, possibly using port scanning (Kaushik, Pilli, and Joshi 2010).

6. *Data exfiltration*: Data is transmitted to external servers controlled by the attacker, via built-in file transfer, FTP, HTTP, the Tor anonymity network, or other methods.

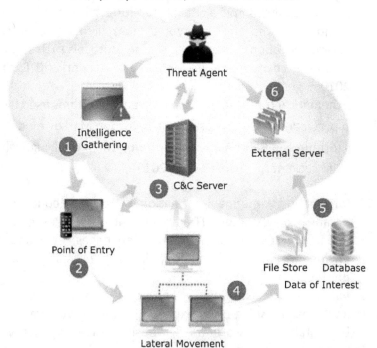

The life cycle proposed by Ghafir et al. (Ghafir et al. 2019), based on the hidden Markov model, in six stages.

Chen et al. propose the following six steps for an APT attack (Z. Chen et al. 2022):

1. *Reconnaissance*: Collecting information (social, hobbies and from social networks (Zimba et al. 2020)) for APT attack and developing attack strategies. Information about the target network infrastructure includes models of network switches, routers, and communication protocols used in the network.
2. *Initial compromise*: Collected information is used to attack the network or exploit its vulnerabilities to gain administrator privileges. The initial compromise targets users (B. Lee, Mahinderjit Singh, and Mohd Shariff 2019) (via phishing messages or links) and network vulnerabilities (including zero-day vulnerabilities to gain root privileges (Nicho and McDermott 2019)).
3. *Lateral movement*: The compromised device is used to obtain legitimate credentials to other computers on the network, through techniques such as pass-the-hash, pass-the-ticket, and remote desktop protocol (Alshamrani et al. 2019).
4. *Pivoting*: Using subnets with domain controllers connected by a communication channel, e.g. a VPN (Apruzzese et al. 2017).
5. *Data exfiltration*: The session established by the attack is used to transmit files. possibly fragmenting the files before transfer, possibly sending different fragments to different DNS servers, connecting them later (Nar and Sastry 2018).
6. *Post-attack stages*: After the attack is completed, it is useful to clean up the traces of the attack to prevent further investigations (Guerra-Manzanares, Nõmm, and Bahsi 2019).

## APT in seven steps

Vukalovic and Delija present a general approach to an APT attack in seven steps (Vukalovic and Delija 2015):

1. *Research*: Publicly available information about the victim is sought.
2. *Preparation*: Plan the initial attack by exploiting vulnerabilities using network scanning for custom exploits.
3. *Intrusion*: The first attack is launched, usually by spear-phishing.
4. *Conquering the network*: Using remote access tools or backdoor to control the system.

5. *Concealment of presence*: The attacker remains hidden and possibly inactive in the network for a long period of time.
6. *Data collection*: Data of interest is sought and transmitted at a slow rate as legitimate traffic.
7. *Access maintenance*: New exploits, remote access tools, and C&C servers are modified or developed to extend network access.

In 2013, Mandiant discussed a 7-stage life cycle model based on their research on alleged Chinese APT attacks between 2004 and 2013 (Mandiant 2013):

1. *Initial compromise*: Through social engineering and email phishing with zero-day exploits, or planting malware on a website where the victim's employees reach.
2. *Foothold establishment*: Installation of malicious software on the victim's network, backdoor and network tunnels for access.
3. *Privilege escalation*: Using exploits and cracking passwords for administrator privileges.
4. *Internal reconnaissance*: Gathering information about infrastructure, trust relationships, domain structure.
5. *Lateral movement*: Extending control to other workstations, servers and infrastructure elements, and collecting data.
6. *Maintaining presence*: Continuous control of access channels and credentials already obtained.
7. *Mission completion*: Depending on the attacker's intentions,

stages 3-6 can be carried out in any order the attacker wants (Alshamrani et al. 2019).

The Lockheed Martin company proposed a seven-stage life cycle called the *cyber kill chain* (CKC) (Lockheed Martin 2023):

1. *Reconnaissance*: A preliminary network reconnaissance using spear-phishing, port scanning and social engineering techniques.
2. *Arming*: A payload is sent to the victim, usually an exploit for a RAT/Trojan delivery.
3. *Delivery*: The payload is sent to the victim via email, websites, or other methods.
4. *Exploit*: The exploit that was sent to the victim is executed.
5. *Installation*: A Trojan and/or RAT is installed.
6. *Command and Control*: Connecting to the attacker's C&C server.
7. *Action*: Data exfiltration compromising data integrity and availability. This stage can take weeks, months or even years.

The Intrusion Kill Chain (IKC) attack model (Hutchins, Cloppert, and Amin 2011) proposes a seven-step framework for detecting and analyzing cyber-attacks, with a layered security architecture and an event collection and analysis of system security:

1. *Information gathering*: Target selection, intelligence gathering, identification of potential vulnerabilities.
2. *Weaponization*: Developing malicious code to explore vulnerabilities through PDF and PPT document files.
3. *Delivery*: Transferring data from the target environment.
4. *Exploitation*: Executing malicious code.
5. *Installation*: RAT remote access allows persistence in the target environment.
6. *Command and Control*: Communication channel for controlling malware and connecting to a C&C server.
7. *Actions*: After completing the objectives by exfiltrating the data (Bhatt, Yano, and Gustavsson 2014).

The US Air Force described an APT attack in 7 steps (Ask 2013) (Adelaiye, Ajibola, and Silas 2019):

1. *Selecting a target organization*: APT attacks are usually initiated by government organizations trying to steal government secrets of other nations (Rowe 2013).
2. *Information gathering*: The weakest link, the human factor as a vulnerability in that organization is considered (Brewer 2014).
3. *Gaining access*: Malware, usually zero-day, is used to access the target network. Alternatively, can be used spear-phishing, watering hole attack, USB etc. (P. Chen, Desmet, and Huygens 2014) (Ghafir and Prenosil 2014)
4. *Exploitation*: Establishing a connection to a command and control (C&C) server, using e.g. port 443 (Ghafir and Prenosil 2014). Legitimate tools and services are used at this stage to reduce possible detection. Commands are given remotely (Marchetti et al. 2016), basically using fast-flow DNS as a technique, preventing the detection of unusual traffic to or from a single destination (Ask 2013).
5. *Operation*: Vulnerable systems are scanned (Ghafir and Prenosil 2014) to gain access to information of interest. In this stage the malware continuously modifies and changes its location to avoid detection, stealing access credentials and escalating system privileges (P. Chen, Desmet, and Huygens 2014).

6. *Discovery and collection of data*: Lateral movement creates a channel of transmission of data located and collected in as few locations as possible for easy exfiltration (Ghafir and Prenosil 2014) (Villeneuve and Bennett 2012).
7. *Data exfiltration*: Data is transferred using secure channels, mainly SSL/TLS, to avoid detection and hide the transmission process (P. Chen, Desmet, and Huygens 2014).

## APT in eight steps

Mandiant (now FireEye), proposed an eight-step model after analyzing the APT1 campaign (Mandiant 2013), as follows:
1. *Initial recognition*: From outside the network,
2. *Initial compromise*: Through, for example, spear-phishing.
3. *Establishing a foothold*: Ensuring control, for example through C&C servers.
4. *Privilege escalation*: Obtaining credentials to access resources.
5. *Internal reconnaissance*: Gathering all information about the victim.
6. *Lateral movement*: Using legitimate credentials to scale.
7. *Maintaining presence*: Actions to remain undetected for a long period of time.
8. *Mission completion*: Information is compressed and possibly fragmented and encrypted to be sent to C&C servers.

## APT in eleven stages

In the eleven-stage model some stages can be developed in parallel with the main stages of the cycle to maintain persistence and to extract information (Quintero-Bonilla and Martín del Rey 2020). ATT and CK analyzes of tactics can be considered as distinct stages of an APT life cycle to meet the strategic objective (Swisscom 2019):
1. *Initial access*: Searching for "patient zero".
2. *Persistence*: Gaining access.
3. *Escalation of privileges*: Installing malware.
4. *Discovery*: Obtaining information of interest.
5. *Lateral movement*: Network expansion.
6. *Collection*: Collection of information of interest.
7. *Exfiltration*: Extracting data. The following steps can be executed in parallel with the previous seven steps:

8. *Execution*: Malware activation through remote connections (between initial access stage and lateral movement).
9. *Concealment*: Avoiding defense and detection (firewall, logs, etc.).
10. *Access to credentials*: Accessing the system with valid credentials.
11. *Command and Control*: Creating a C&C channel for remote communication.

## Consequences of APT attacks

The main negative consequences of APT attacks:
1. *Data leaks*: APTs can lead to massive data theft, exposing sensitive information and causing reputational damage to organizations.
2. *Economic impact*: The economic consequences of APT attacks can be severe, resulting in financial losses, lawsuits, and regulatory fines.
3. *Threat to national security*: APT targeting critical infrastructure or government institutions can pose a significant threat to national security.

Due to the large number of recent APT attacks on organizations, IT budgets end up increasing significantly (Swisscom 2019). According to Trend research, the most targeted industry for spear phishing APT attacks is governments, with an attack rate of 65%, which is almost double the second ranked target industry with an attack rate of 35% (Mandiant 2013). Most APTs are created by governments because of the complexity, time, sophistication, and resources required (P. Chen, Desmet, and Huygens 2014).

# DEFENSE STRATEGIES

Traditional security technology and methods are ineffective in detecting or mitigating APTs. There are tens of millions of malware variants (Messier 2013), making it extremely difficult to protect organizations from APTs. Command and control network traffic can be detected with sophisticated methods. Deep log analyzes and their correlation are of limited utility. It's a challenge to separate noise from legitimate traffic. Active cyber defense is more effective against APTs. Human-Introduced Cyber Vulnerabilities (HICV) are one of the biggest problems, constituting a significant attack vector (Merz 2019). The main measures that can be taken against APT attacks are:

1. *Network monitoring and anomaly detection*: Implementing robust network monitoring and anomaly detection systems can help identify APT activity in its early stages.
2. *Employee training and awareness*: Educating employees about APT risks, particularly through phishing awareness programs, can help prevent successful attacks.
3. *Patch management*: Regularly updating and patching software and systems can mitigate the risk of APT exploiting known vulnerabilities.
4. *Endpoint security*: Using strong endpoint security solutions can detect and prevent malware and other APT-related threats.

A United States Department of Defense Joint Chiefs of Staff methodology (Smart 2011), the Kill Chain, is considered a guideline for cyber targeting in five key areas: (1) positive target identification, (2 ) location of targets, (3) attack assignment, (4) capability/target pairing, and (5) assessment of potential collateral damage. According to Smart, an updated "JP 3-60" approach should "introduce the concepts of an *adversary's cyber center of gravity* and a *cyberspace joint operations area*. An adversary's cyber presence consists of computers, information systems, hardware, online personas, and so forth, which may be geographically separated from his physical center of gravity. Once planners identify the cyber center of gravity (a critical point—a source of power for the adversary's cyber operations), they can target it." (Smart 2011, 72)

Hutchins et al. argue that an effective defense against APTs must emphasize systems resilience through performance and effectiveness against cyberattacks (Hutchins, Cloppert, and Amin 2011).

Bere et al. state that the best defense is through risk assessment, implementation of policies and control, awareness campaigns and monitoring and evaluation, with emphasis on awareness campaigns, through specific policies (Bere et al. 2015). They approach the SANS model of security awareness (Russell 2002). Another model focuses on reducing the threat of phishing by influencing behavior (Arachchilage and Love 2014). Awareness promotion focuses on positively influencing behavior and reducing the threat to security (Russell 2002).

Adelaiye, Ajibola, and Silas highlight several techniques to mitigate APT by reducing the adverse effect of unwanted events (Adelaiye, Ajibola, and Silas 2019):

1. *Anomaly detection*: Using a model of normal behavior for comparison with real behavior (Mahadevan et al. 2010). Anomaly detection includes the detection of network traffic and suspicious activity or "irregular" clusters of activity (potentially

obtained through machine learning). Several researchers propose the use of big data analytics for APT detection (P. Giura and Wang 2012).

2. *Whitelists*: When access is allowed only a few trusted entities have access (Huh et al. 2011).

3. *Blacklists*: A list of known malicious applications and processes (can only prevent pre-known attack types) (Edwards et al. 2012).

4. *Intrusion detection systems (IDS)*: They are based on the analysis of ports, protocols, IP addresses, system events, system calls, etc., generating alerts (García-Teodoro et al. 2009).

5. *Awareness*: Attackers exploit the human factor in the security chain (Pfleeger, Sasse, and Furnham 2014), assessing, at the same time, the level of knowledge and understanding of security (Bulgurcu, Cavusoglu, and Benbasat 2010). According to an APT awareness survey (ISACA 2016), more than half of industries are unaware of the differences between APTs and traditional threats, and 67% of respondents report a lack of APT awareness training.

6. *Deception*: Through devices that hide the true identity, the attacker is made to believe that he has succeeded by being granted access to a fake system to keep him busy until he is identified (Nance and Bishop 2017).

7. *Cryptography*: Changing information in a format that cannot be understood (Peikert 2016).

8. *Traffic/data analysis*: Use of statistical methods for analysis (Conti et al. 2015).

9. *SIEM*: Security Information and Event Management (SIEM) tool collects data for analysis of potential attacks (Coppolino et al. 2012). A data loss prevention solution can be implemented as the last line of defense (Schmid, Hill, and Ghosh 2002).

10. *Pattern recognition*: Detection by recognition based on mode of operation (Wright et al. 2010).

11. *Risk assessment*: By monitoring application activities and aggregating impact and risk (Lo and Chen 2012).

12. *Multi-layer security*: Communication on different layers with various uses, combining several of the above methods implemented in the network plane, application plane, user plane, physical plane, etc. (Moon et al. 2014)

Malware is critical to the initial intrusion, especially zero-day exploits or custom evasion tools. The ability to detect advanced malware is important to defend against APTs. Sandboxing is a proven technique for analyzing unknown advanced malware behavior (Rafique et al. 2014). It must also be taken into account that advanced malware can resort to sandbox evasion techniques (Singh and Bu 2014).

Ghafir and Prenosil proposed adding functions to an open source intrusion detection system, which would include data traffic analysis based on sent requests and protocols used, filtering using blacklists and using the hash algorithm in protecting confidentiality and data integrity (Ghafir and Prenosil 2016).

Wang et al. proposed a gene-based approach in detecting advanced persistent threats using the pattern of pre-existing attacks (Y. Wang et al. 2014).

According to Adelaiye, Ajibola, and Silas, 72% of researchers combined several methods to mitigate the threat, considering traditional methods to be ineffective. Among the methods adopted, traffic/data analysis is the most widely used, followed by anomaly detection, pattern recognition and multilayer security. Ideally, at least two methods should be combined. As the second method, the most used was traffic/data analysis followed by pattern recognition (Adelaiye, Ajibola, and Silas 2019).

Rot and Olszewski believe that the most successful form of defense against APTs is constant monitoring and reaction to as many APTs as possible (Rot and Olszewski 2017). In 76% of cases, antivirus software was not an obstacle to APT attacks (Deloitte 2016), so traditional protection is not enough. Basically, any effective APT defense approach must include defense in depth, a detection capability, an APT incident response plan, a recovery plan, and security awareness and training (Ashford 2011). Each stage of APT is well known and easy to counter. The problems arise with their combination, with customization for a specific target.

Intelligence-based defense is a strategy that leverages knowledge about adversaries and adapts defenses based on gathered information (Hutchins, Cloppert, and Amin 2011). Defenders can create an information feedback loop to identify patterns of previous intrusion attempts, try to understand adversary techniques, and then implement specific countermeasures.

The main types of APT defenses are hardware- and cloud-based (Rot 2016). Hardware-based solutions involve a dedicated device that monitors suspicious traffic based on reputation indices and does behavioral analysis and sandboxing. They have some limitations; they are not able to record all network traffic. Cloud-based solutions, provided as a multi-user platform, should avoid these limitations, and monitor traffic more effectively, performing a holistic analysis (behavior, vulnerabilities, address filtering, SSL transmission monitoring, active content, etc.). The most effective are the stratified protection models (Rot and Olszewski 2017):

1. *Multi-Layered APT Protection Model*: It is based on defense in depth, which involves careful protection of each layer of the network: people, devices, and applications (Hudson 2013).
2. *SIEM platform as a form of defense against attacks*: The implementation of second-generation SIEM (Security Information and Event Management) tools for managing security and incident information. SIEMs provide "data collection and archiving, detailed event and normalization analysis, reports, queries, and usually some form of real-time analytics" (Muszyński and Shipley 2008).
3. *Big data technology in APT detection and resistance*: Also called second-generation SIEM, through an integrated log analysis and anomaly detection based on a typical pattern customized for a specific organization (Kim et al. 2015) or behavioral analysis. Solutions based on MapReduce, Hadoop or Hive allow the analysis time to be shortened by approximately twenty times (Zions Bancorporation 2012)

Defending against an APT attack cannot be done with a single tool (Alshamrani et al. 2019). Event correlation plays a key role in defense in depth by adopting multiple layers of defense. L. Yang et al. modeled by defining the balance of the cyber network as a security measure, studied and theoretically analyzed other factors on this balance and reported that the balance security of a cyber network will decrease with the addition of new edges to the network (Yang et al. 2017). Equilibrium security reaches its maximum when prevention resources are close to that of recovery resources and the same value increases with the increase of defense resources per unit of time. They recommend distributing defense resources equally between prevention and recovery and suggest that configuring multiple resources is effective in protecting against APTs.

Different defense methods that can be used against APT, are (Alshamrani et al. 2019):

1. **Monitoring methods**
   a. *Disk monitoring*: By antivirus, firewall or content filtering, and CPU monitoring for each of these systems.
   b. *Memory monitoring*: For detecting malware that can run in system memory rather than from a file, avoiding traces (Virvilis and Gritzalis 2013). Duqu 2.0, which infested Kaspersky labs in 2015 (Kaspersky 2015), ran this way.
   c. *Packet monitoring*: Communication with the Command-and-Control Center when the system is compromised

and for data transfer helps identify suspicious behaviors (Marchetti et al. 2016).

    d. *Code monitoring*: Code bugs are vulnerabilities through which attackers can penetrate systems. These can be identified by static analysis techniques such as Taint analysis and data flow analysis.

    e. *Log monitoring*: Can help detect or prevent attacks in the early stages by correlating logs (Shalaginov, Franke, and Huang 2016).

**2. Detection methods**

    a. *Anomaly detection*: Anomaly detection techniques to detect different stages of APT attacks.

       i. Approaches and methods (Hodge and Austin 2004)

       ii. Application in APT detection (Kim et al. 2015): AI/ML techniques correlated with different APT stages that can be detected using AI/ML techniques:

          1. Spear phishing

          2. Malicious DNS domains

          3. User profiling

          4. Monitoring data in motion

          5. Abnormal behavior:

    b. *Pattern matching*: Uses regular intrusion detection and prevention systems (Yan and Zhang 2013).

**3. Mitigation methods**

    a. *Reactive methods*: Identify possible attack scenarios based on the present vulnerabilities

       i. Graphical analysis (J. Johnson and Hogan 2013)

    b. *Proactive methods*: Techniques that can deceive the attacker or change the attack surface

       i. Honeypot and Honeynet strategies (Bowen et al. 2009)

       ii. Defending the moving target (Crouse, Prosser, and Fulp 2015).

Due to the specific characteristics of APT, there is no single effective protection solution. Current best practice is a wide range of security countermeasures that result in a multi-layered defense. Some of the existing defense systems need to be redesigned to work in the APT context. P. Chen, Desmet, and Huygens offers a comparison of different APTs and attack techniques and countermeasures at each stage of an APT attack (P. Chen, Desmet, and Huygens 2014).

# RELATED WORKS

Lately the number of APT attacks has increased rapidly, and numerous security incidents have been reported. Adversaries often exploit the fact that most protection efforts go into perimeter protection, neglecting the interior of the infrastructure (Tankard 2011), for example, the demilitarized zone (DMZ), but the intensity of surveillance is limited. Specialized intrusion detection or intrusion prevention tools require a large amount of administrative and human resources to monitor the output of these systems. Detection of APT attacks has become the subject of extensive research. Logging engines (e.g. syslog) or log management solutions (e.g. Graylog) are useful, but detecting events in these log files is insufficient. In this idea, AECID (Automatic Event Correlation for Incident Detection) (Friedberg and Fiedler 2014) applies whitelists and monitors the events in the system and the interdependence between the different systems, being able to obtain an overview of the "normal" behavior of the infrastructure (Rass, König, and Schauer 2017).

Rass, König, and Schauer (Rass, König, and Schauer 2017) consider game theory as a natural tool for analyzing conflicts of interest in the case of APT (van Dijk et al. 2013) which, together with agent-based models (Busby, Onggo, and Liu 2016), can be applied for risk analysis and quantification. He also discusses matrix games as a suitable model to explain what the victim can do against an APT (Hamilton et al. 2002) and proposes a new form of capturing payoff uncertainty in game-theory models.

Investigating hacker communities (Alshamrani et al. 2019) (from dark-web forums) (Nunes et al. 2016) can help identify zero-day vulnerabilities before they are exploited. Research in this field has the potential to have a high social impact (Benjamin, Li, and Holt 2015).

In Vukalovic and Delija (Vukalovic and Delija 2015), the authors discussed educating users and implementing stricter policies and static rules to detect anomalies.

In Ussath et al. (Ussath et al. 2016), the authors analyzed several reports and concluded that spear-phishing is the most common approach chosen for initial compromise, and credential stripping is the most common method for lateral movement.

Chen and Desmet (P. Chen, Desmet, and Huygens 2014) studied APT attacks, countermeasures to be taken, and some APT detection methods.

Tankard et al. (Tankard 2011) studied APT attacks and explained the different stages of attacks and detection techniques, including monitoring methods to detect APT in a huge network.

# CASE STUDIES

Real-world case studies provide valuable insight into successful and unsuccessful APT detection scenarios. Analyzing the incidents and the corresponding detection methods applied allows a deeper understanding of the challenges and constitute lessons for combating APT.

APTs began in the national security sectors, but have expanded their scope to non-governmental commercial and financial sectors. Symantec, in its 2018 Internet Security Threat Report, Volume 23 (Symantec 2018a), states that APTs use ransomware as an attack tool. Alshamrani et al. (Alshamrani et al. 2019) details the main APT attacks known to date:

## Titan Rain

In 2003, a series of coordinated cyber-attacks infiltrated multiple computers and networks at US defense facilities. They continued until the end of 2015, stealing unclassified information using deception and the use of multiple attack vectors (Alshamrani et al. 2019). Hackers in China led the Titan Rain campaign against US government targets in an attempt to steal sensitive state secrets. The attackers targeted military data and launched APT attacks on top systems of government agencies, including NASA and the FBI. Security analysts have pointed to the Chinese People's Liberation Army as the source of the attacks.

## Sykipot

The Sykipot APT malware exploits flaws in Adobe Reader and Acrobat. It was detected in 2006 and continued until 2013. The Sykipot malware family was used in APT as part of a long-running series of cyber-attacks, mainly targeting organizations in the US and UK, using a spear phishing attack with malicious links and attachments that contained zero-day exploits (Yasar and Rosencrance 2021).

## GhostNet

The GhostNet attack was discovered in 2009, being executed from China via spear phishing messages, compromising computers in over 100 countries. Government ministries and embassies were targeted, turning them into listening and recording sources by remotely turning on cameras and audio recording capabilities (BBC 2009).

## Stuxnet

Stuxnet was launched in 2009, a sophisticated worm aimed at thwarting Iran's nuclear project. It used XOR encryption with a static key (OxFF) to decrypt parts of the payload and a fixed 32-byte key to encrypt the data it sent to the C&C server, again using an XOR algorithm (Virvilis and Gritzalis 2013). It exploited a zero-day vulnerability found in Windows Explorer's LNK file. Microsoft named it Stuxnet, a combination of filenames found in the malicious code (.stub and MrxNet.sys). It was later discovered that he also used a vulnerability in the printer spooler of Windows computers, spreading to all computers that shared the printer, and vulnerabilities in the Windows keyboard file and the Task Scheduler file to gain full control through privilege escalation. He used a password encoded in a Siemens Step7 software to infect database servers with Step7 and from there other connected machines. After the first intrusion, it sends the internal IP and public IP of that system along with the computer name, operating system, and Siemens Step7 information to one of 2 command servers in 2 different countries. The malware infected the system and updated itself with new functionality. Later, other computers in several countries were infected (Langner 2011). Stuxnet used 4 zero-day vulnerabilities, 2 stolen certificates and 2 command and control centers. Smart and layered, it could be modified by attackers through command-and-control centers using over 400 elements in its configuration file. Its activity ended in 2012, slowing down the process of generating nuclear weapons (Alshamrani et al. 2019).

## Operation Aurora

Operation Aurora was launched in 2009 targeting various commercial companies using the Hydraq Trojan. It used multiple malware components encrypted in multiple layers. Google, which announced this attack, was one of the victims, followed by Adobe. The name "Aurora" comes from the malware injected during its compilation on the attackers' machine, using a zero-day exploit in Internet Explorer (Ferrer and Ferrer 2010) to establish a foothold. One of the components created a backdoor, allowing access to the network. Previously, the malware had exploited a vulnerability in the Adobe Reader and Acrobat applications. The attacks continued for several months in different countries around the globe under different variants of the Hydraq Trojan. The malware gathers system and network information and collects usernames and passwords in a file then sent to the command and control center with an encrypted IP or domain name (Alshamrani et al. 2019).

# Duque

Duqu was detected in September 2011, but has been active since February 2010. It has similarities with Stuxnet, but different objective (espionage) (Bencsáth et al. 2012). He infected approx. 50 targets worldwide. After the initial infection, it remained active for 30 days before self-destructing. The initial infection and propagation were through Microsoft Word files containing the zero-day True Type font parsing vulnerability. The program connected to servers via 80/TCP and 443/TCP ports and used a custom C&C protocol. Duqu used shorthand by encoding and appending the transferred data to JPEG image files (Virvilis and Gritzalis 2013).

# RSA SecureID attack

In 2011, EMC Software's RSA cyberattack compromised information associated with SecureID, a two-factor authentication token. The intrusion was aided by phishing sent to the company's employees with Excel files attached, through a zero-day exploit to Adobe flash player installing a backdoor (Alshamrani et al. 2019).

# Flame

Flame was first detected by chance in May 2012 (Bencsáth et al. 2012) but is believed to have been active for 5-8 years already. It has an unusual size of about 20 MB. It infested thousands of Windows systems, especially in the Middle East. The attackers had to perform a complex cryptanalytic attack (chosen prefix collision attack for the MD5 algorithm) against the licensing certification authority for Microsoft Terminal Services. Flame has used over 80 domains as C&C servers. Communication was performed via HTTP, HTTPS or SSH, using XOR encryption and RC4 algorithm (Virvilis and Gritzalis 2013).

# Carbanak

Carbanak was an attack to steal money from financial institutions, started in 2013, using spear-phishing, with files attacked exploiting Microsoft Office vulnerabilities. It remained undetected until early 2014 (A. Johnson 2016). After establishing a foothold by installing the backdoor, internal reconnaissance was done as part of their lateral movement, communicating with the attackers' C&C server via a custom binary protocol. Carbanak slowed down in 2015 but continued until 2017 in different variants (Alshamrani et al. 2019).

# Red October

Red October was discovered in October 2012 but has been active since May 2007, targeting diplomatic, governmental, and scientific institutions (SecureList 2013). With a minimalist architecture, it succeeded in stealing information from mobile phones by being installed as a plugin for Office and Adobe reader applications. It used XOR encryption to wrap its main executable and encrypt the exfiltrated data.

## Other APT attacks

According to (Yasar and Rosencrance 2021):

APT28, also known as Fancy Bear, Pawn Storm, Sofacy Group, and Sednit, was identified by Trend Micro researchers in 2014 as attacking military and government targets in Eastern Europe, including Ukraine and Georgia, as well as campaigns targeting NATO organizations and US defense contractors.

APT29 (Russian group Cozy Bear) used spear phishing attacks since 2015 on the Pentagon, since 2016 on the Democratic National Committee.

APT34 (Iran) was identified in 2017 by FireEye researchers but has been active since 2014. It targeted companies in the Middle East.

APT37 (also known as Reaper, StarCruft, and Group), is an advanced persistent threat linked to North Korea that is believed to have emerged around 2012, using spear phishing attacks exploiting an Adobe Flash zero-day vulnerability.

## Common characteristics

Virvilis, Gritzalis, and Apostolopoulos (Virvilis, Gritzalis, and Apostolopoulos 2013) identified common features (techniques, exploits, functionalities) that can allow malware to avoid detection:

1. *Operating system and architecture targeted*: 32-bit versions of Windows (no malware would run on 64-bit systems), especially when targeting kernel components. But since attackers had access to valid certificates (Stuxnet, Duqu) to sign on 64-bit, the main reason for 32-bit might be that most victims use this architecture.

2. *Initial attack vectors*: Duqu and Red October used Word and Excel documents to infect their targets, while MiniDuke exploited Adobe's PDF Reader. In Stuxnet and Flame the initial likely infection method was via removable drives or watering hole attacks. With Office 2010 Suite, Microsoft introduced

"protected view" as an additional protection. Thus, it is assumed that victims who got infected were running outdated versions of MS Office or had security features disabled. MiniDuke was able to exploit all versions of Adobe Reader and bypass the sandbox.

3. *Command execution and privilege escalation*: All programs used zero-day exploits for command or privilege escalation.

4. *Network access.*: Communications were made through ports 80/TCP, 443/TCP or 22/TCP, used for outbound traffic with HTTP, HTTPS and SSH protocols, additionally using encryption/obfuscation and compression. Most of the victims had very relaxed Internet access restrictions.

5. *Network IDs and endpoint antivirus products*: Stuxnet, Flame, Duqu, and MiniDuke avoided antivirus software. Flame, Duqu, Red October, and MiniDuke encrypted or avoided their own network traffic to "fly under the radar" by avoiding network intrusion detection systems (NIDS). The shortcomings of such protection systems are well known (Denault et al. 1994), but they are still the most common toolkits in use.

6. *Use of encryption/avoidance*: All attacks relied on XOR "encryption" to avoid detection and complicated malware analysis, and to protect configuration files and transmitted traffic. Duqu and Flame additionally used AES and RC4 algorithms respectively.

7. *Digital signature exploitation*: Stuxnet and Duqu were digitally signed using compromised digital certificates. Flame exploited the collision resistance of the MD5 hash function and replicated it through the WSUS service.

## OPPORTUNITIES AND CHALLENGES

Countries and organizations should work together to share threat intelligence, helping to identify and respond to more effective APT campaigns. The development of international legal frameworks to address APT can enable the monitoring and prosecution of threat actors.

APT tactics continue to evolve, requiring continuous adaptation of cybersecurity strategies. Integrating artificial intelligence and machine learning into cybersecurity solutions is becoming increasingly vital in the fight against APTs.

The nature of APT attacks is itself a challenge, due to specific characteristics of these attacks: determined and powerful attackers, long duration of attacks, vulnerabilities of internal employees exploited through social engineering and bad infrastructure when the environment uses cloud computing resources.

APT has several specific characteristics that make it more difficult to detect (Marchetti et al. 2016):

- *Unbalanced data*: Weak signals among huge amounts of data; unlike botnets (Feily, Shahrestani, and Ramadass 2009), in APT only a few hosts are infected.
- *Base rate problem*: Rare events that extend over very long periods of time (Axelsson 2000).
- *Lack of publicly available data*: Most victim companies have no interest in publishing details of such events.
- *Use of encryption and standard protocols*: Prevents the effectiveness of network security solutions (Denning 1987).

# OBSERVATIONS ON APT ATTACKS

APTs are sophisticated, specific, and evolving threats, but certain patterns can be identified in their process. Traditional countermeasures are not sufficient to protect against APTs. Potential victims must gain a basic understanding of the steps and techniques involved in attacks, on which to develop specific capabilities.

In APT mitigation, game theory can play an important role as a model of the competition between a defender and an attacker (Rass, König, and Schauer 2017). Uncertainty elements can be addressed with notions such as stochastic games or games of incomplete information, or simpler and easier to configure matrix game model that considers time to be discrete for the attacker but continuous for the defender. The game-theoretic perspective allows the development of an optimal defense strategy starting almost directly from the available information, avoiding opponent modeling.

Technologies such as deep learning, a new approach to network security, constant monitoring, adaptation, and experiential learning can be used in protection against APTs (SignalSense 2015). PwC, in its 2015 Global State of Information Security Survey, notes that within organizations, current (31%) or former (27%) employees are the primary source of insider threats (PWC 2014). More attention should also be paid to traffic monitoring based on neural networks (scalable detectors, host classification, IP, packets and traffic reputation) looking for anomalies from the usual pattern. In general, protection strategies include, according to (Rot and Olszewski 2017), integrated information exchange between security points, advanced prevention and detection, including a broad strategic approach (tactical hardware configuration and attack scenarios), SSL traffic monitoring and ensuring full protection.

An APT can be considered one of the most concerning security issues, in which IoT (Internet of Things) occupies a leading place. Despite the evolution of APT, some traditional approaches or models can still be used to detect or identify such attacks. Based on network behavior, one can monitor the network for suspicious activity and take proactive action.

The most common way to gain initial access to networks is through social engineering, via spear phishing emails to employees. Therefore, organizations need to improve their user awareness programs; the human aspect of APT is very complex and needs to be approached from a behavioral perspective as well as behavioral theories of motivated action.

Commonly used machine learning techniques and models to detect an APT attack are SVM, k-NN and DT with good results. It is recommended to create a dataset containing network flows (normal and malicious) to train the ML algorithms used in the framework, and the effectiveness of the framework can be tested by simulating an APT attack in a controlled space (Quintero-Bonilla and Martín del Rey 2020).

# 3 APT DETECTION

Advanced persistent threats (APTs) pose a formidable challenge to cyber security, characterized by their sophisticated and persistent nature. Advanced persistent threats are a significant cybersecurity issue of concern today, posing serious risks to organizations, governments, and individuals.

Detecting an APT in progress mainly involves the malware detection methods already introduced. The biggest problem with zero-day exploit malware in the case of APT is that there is no signature in the databases. Malicious code is polymorphic and customized for a given target or dynamically modified during the attack. APT detection involves online analysis, real-time reporting, and correlated log analysis to recognize and neutralize a potential threat.

Recent security incidents, such as Operation Aurora (McAfee 2010b) Operation Shady RAT (Alperovitch 2011), Operation Red October (SecureList 2013) or MiniDuke (MITRE 2021), have demonstrated that current security mechanisms are insufficient to detect and stop targeted and personalized attacks. These advanced attacks raise the question of whether it is even possible to prevent intrusions with reasonable certainty.

An interesting concept for detecting APTs is exploiting the usually unnoticed relationships between different applications and components of a network, with many experts arguing that these relationships are the main weakness exploited by attackers to compromise systems (for example, the same passwords for multiple services or standard architecture). Assessing these relationships by correlating events across the network allows the automatic generation of a system behavior model that describes common events and their relationships (Friedberg et al. 2015).

## Features of advanced persistent threats

APTs are characterized by their stealthy, protracted, and targeted nature. Actors behind APTs use advanced techniques such as zero-day exploits, social engineering, and polymorphic malware to remain undetected for long periods of time. Understanding these characteristics is crucial for the development of effective detection mechanisms.

There are certain symptoms of APT attacks, including (Yasar and Rosencrance 2021):

1. Unusual activity in user accounts
2. Detection of Trojan backdoor malware for access through unusual database activity
3. Presence of unusual data files
4. Anomalies in output data.

## Evolution of APT tactics

As technology advances, so do the tactics used by APTs. The evolving strategies of APTs include the use of artificial intelligence, machine learning, and encrypted communication channels to evade traditional detection measures. Examining these tactics is vital to staying in the ongoing game between defenders and threat actors.

According to Zou et al. (Zou et al. 2020), current approaches to bottom-up APT detection (e.g., provenance - flow of information) attempt to infer the existence of APT tactics from low-level information. APT5,6,7,8 detection is mainly based on unsupervised "connecting the dots" through provenance tracking. These approaches first perform activity dependency analysis and causality graph construction, then use heuristics to simplify the resulting graphs by analyzing them. One of the disadvantages of this approach is the problem of dependency explosion, well known in digital forensics.

Top-down approaches take advantage of knowledge of known APTs by circumventing the dependency explosion problem. They are based on patterns of operation of some APTs, such as Stuxnet, without the need for unsupervised association learning. For example, HOLMES uses the APT lifecycle as an attack model and then tries to match each step (Milajerdi et al. 2019). HOLMES collects computer audit data and ranks the severity of APT attacks in real time, considering seven stages of the so-called "kill chain".

# WAYS TO DETECT APT

## Traffic analytics

Brewer (Brewer 2014) and Virvilis and Gritzalis (Virvilis and Gritzalis 2013) describe and analyze cases of known APTs: Stuxnet, Duqu and Flame. In Giura and Wang (Paul Giura and Wang 2012), the authors propose an attack pyramid that aims to identify the movements of an attacker. De Vries et al. (De Vries et al. 2012) propose possible building blocks for an APT detection framework. Johnson and Hogan (J. Johnson and Hogan 2013), based on graph analysis, propose a new metric for measuring the vulnerability of a network environment. In Friedberg et al. (Friedberg et al. 2015) an anomaly detection system is proposed for identifying APTs from multiple logs. Sasaki (Sasaki 2011) focuses on data exfiltration detection. Bertino et al. (Bertino and Ghinita 2011) focus on the analysis of Database Management System (DBMS) access logs to detect suspicious patterns for possible exfiltration. Liu et al. (Liu et al. 2009) propose a framework for data exfiltration detection by analyzing network communications through automatic signature generation. A botnet is a large set of distributed compromised hosts controlled by one or more command and control servers. Gu et al. (Gu et al. 2008) proposed the detection of infected hosts and command and control servers related to botnet activities. Azaria et al. (Azaria et al. 2014) research insider threats; Greitzer and Frincke (Greitzer and Frincke 2010) focus for this purpose on host-based logs, and Bowen et al. (Bowen et al. 2009) on honey jar strategies. There are several statistical approaches for anomaly detection (Chandola, Banerjee, and Kumar 2009), such as those based on thresholding (Soong 2004), clustering (Hartigan 1975), or based on the boxplot rule (Soong 2004).

Marchetti et al. (Marchetti et al. 2016) proposes an APT detection approach to analyze large volumes of network traffic to reveal weak signals related to data exfiltration and other suspicious activities. Finally, a ranking of the most suspicious internal hosts is obtained, for early APT detection, a model aimed at detecting APT-related activities, and a set of algorithms for assessing suspicion. The life cycle adopted by Marchetti is that of Brewer (Brewer 2014), which identifies five main phases: recognition; compromise; maintaining access; lateral movement; and data exfiltration. Each phase has particular characteristics with records in the traffic logs. Its framework is able to identify and classify suspicious hosts possibly involved in APT-related data exfiltration based only on network traffic data, ultimately yielding a classified list of suspicious hosts possibly involved in data exfiltration and other APT-related activities.

## Technological approaches to APT detection

Advances in technology have paved the way for innovative approaches to APT detection.

Friedberg et al. (Friedberg et al. 2015) study anomaly detection by event correlation, extending common security mechanisms - especially "packet-level" IDS - to improve their results. The approach exploits log files by building a model while processing the input, using search patterns (random substrings of processed lines, to classify information), event classes (classifies log lines using the set of known patterns), hypotheses (possible implications on basis of classification), and rules (proven hypotheses).

# Integrating data science and artificial intelligence

Integrating data science and artificial intelligence applications into APT threat defense is essential in the fight against APT. Application of artificial intelligence (AI) inspired by artificial immune system (AIS) (Jia, Lin, and Ma 2015), deep learning (DL) (McDermott, Majdani, and Petrovski 2018) and machine learning (ML) algorithm (Ghafir, Hammoudeh, et al. 2018) in APT intrusion detection has attracted more research attention.

Chen et al. lists several studies based on data science and artificial intelligence, as follows (Z. Chen et al. 2022):

**Supervised machine learning**: Rachmadi, Mandala, and Oktaria (Rachmadi, Mandala, and Oktaria 2021) introduce an IDS based on the Adaboost model for detecting DoS attacks. Wahla et al. (Wahla et al. 2019) present a framework with Adaboost for detection of low class DoS (LRDoS) attacks. A k-nearest neighbor (KNN) algorithm is proposed for implementation by Manhas and Kotwal (Manhas and Kotwal 2021) to detect multiple network attacks, by using multiple ML algorithms, including KNN MLP, DT, NB and SVM model, to detect IDS. The linear regression (LR) algorithm is studied in Montgomery, Peck, and Vining (Montgomery, Peck, and Vining 2012), and the RF algorithm in ensemble ML consisting of a number of decision trees is proposed by (Probst, Wright, and Boulesteix 2019). The study in (Hasan et al. 2019) uses several ML algorithms including SVM to detect attacks.

**Deep learning**: The Deep AutoEncoder (DAE) consists of two multilayer symmetric feedforward networks, proposed by (C. Zhang et al. 2021). Deep Belief Networks (DBNs) are a class of deep neural networks, which use probability and unsupervised learning to produce results, suggested by (Hinton 2009). Lin, Chen, and Yan (Lin, Chen, and Yan 2013) proposed a fully connected network (FCN) containing fully connected layers where all inputs in a layer are connected to every activation unit in the previous layer. A recurrent neural network (RNN), which takes sequence data as input and performs recursion in the direction of sequence evolution, is studied by Probst, Wright, and Boulesteix (Probst, Wright, and Boulesteix 2019). Long Short-Term Memory (LSTM) is a special type of RNN proposed by Hochreiter and Schmidhuber (Hochreiter and Schmidhuber 1997).

**Unsupervised machine learning**: Density-Based Spatial Clustering with Noise Applications (DBSCAN), a well-known method for clustering samples based on their density and identifying outliers located in low-density areas, is studied by Schubert et al. (Schubert et al. 2017). The K-means clustering algorithm in a vector quantization method in signal processing is addressed by Al-Yaseen, Othman, and Nazri (Al-Yaseen, Othman, and Nazri 2017).

**IoT dataset**: Private IoT datasets are generated and applied for security research in several works. Roldán et al. (Roldán et al. 2020) extract the samples from a normal network scheme to generate a dataset for ML algorithms. The study by Amouri, Alaparthy, and Morgera (Amouri, Alaparthy, and Morgera 2020) implements dedicated sniffer to assemble network traffic in a designed network based on open systems interconnection. Wang and Lu (Xiali Wang and Lu 2020) first created an anomalous dataset of collected frame calls. The study by Park, Li, and Hong (Park, Li, and Hong 2020) uses a composite dataset with host features and flow features that collect sensor data, network traffic, and system resource logs from a smart factory. In Haddadpajouh et al. (Haddadpajouh et al. 2018), the authors separately introduce the creation of a private dataset for benign and malicious attacks.

Sim et al. (Sim, Hart, and Paechter 2014) applied the combination of the immune metaphor and genetic programming in their paper, "Network for Lifelong Learning (NELLI) System", a first step towards creating L2O systems that continue to adapt in time. NELLI independently generates a group of optimization algorithms that has the ability to solve a diverse range of problem instances. The adaptation of the artificial immune system combined with the integration of optimized continuous machine learning approaches to predict attack instances offers great potential to pre-generate algorithms in anticipation of future demand (Eke, Petrovski, and Ahriz 2019).

Eke, Petrovski, and Ahriz investigated the application of ensemble-optimized stacked RNNs for deep learning and their variants as inspired by the Life-Long Learning Optimizer (L2O) approach to improve performance in Intrusion Detection System (IDS). They propose a novel approach using deep neural networks for multi-step APT detection, conducting a series of experiments to evaluate the ability of this model (Eke, Petrovski, and Ahriz 2019).

Quintero-Bonilla and Martín del Rey (Quintero-Bonilla and Martín del Rey 2020) talk about a new system based on machine learning called MLAPT, also presented by Ghafir et al. (Ghafir, Hammoudeh, et al. 2018) that detected APT attacks through early alerts that are analyzed by ML algorithms, which work in three phases: threat detection, alert correlation, and attack prediction. Also a distributed framework architecture for APT detection (DFA-AD) is described in Sharma et al. (Sharma et al. 2017), which classifies events in a distributed environment and correlates them to detect the techniques used by APT, in three phases: the traffic flow is collected, processed and analyzed by recognition using machine learning algorithms; correlate the events generated in the previous phase to be evaluated, create a voting system for information; and potentially generating alerts in the event of an APT attack. Siddiqui et al. presented a fractal-based anomaly classification mechanism using k-NN and fractal dimension of correlation (FD) as anomaly classification algorithms to test the dataset and compare the results (Siddiqui et al. 2016). Shenwen, Yingbo, and Xiongjie study an APT detection system based on the process of big data architecture, using k-NN algorithms with big data, in four stages: data correlation, big data processing with a cluster Hadoop, APT analysis to detect attacks from vulnerabilities and suspicious connections, and APT detection using the Mahout tool (Shenwen, Yingbo, and Xiongjie 2015). Bai et al. addressed anomalies for detecting malicious RDP (remote desktop protocol) sessions (Bai et al. 2019). Zhang et al. propose an attack scenario method on IDS security logs using the KCI (kill chain intrusion) model in four phases: information gathering, intrusion, latent expansion, and information theft (R. Zhang et al. 2017). The most used algorithms in these models were k-NN, SVM and DT (Quintero-Bonilla and Martín del Rey 2020).

Ghafir et al. propose a new intrusion detection system for APT detection and prediction, in two main phases: attack scenario reconstruction, and attack decoding using hidden Markov model (HMM) to determine the sequence more likely of APT stages (Ghafir et al. 2019). Additionally, a prediction algorithm is developed to predict the next step of the APT campaign. The Hidden Markov Model (HMM) is also used in Mandiant to train models using observed network traffic under normal network conditions and to detect deviant sequences of traffic observations (Mandiant 2013). HMM addresses the challenge of providing complete information about the attack campaign. Ghafir et al. propose a novel IDS for APT detection and prediction, using the Viterbi algorithm to determine the most likely sequence of APT steps. APT stage forecasting reveals the APT lifecycle in its early stages, and also helps in understanding the attacker's strategies and objectives.

Al-Saraireh and Masarweh describe a methodology for architecture of an APT detection model, in several steps: data collection and preprocessing, dataset classification, and use of an ML detection model to test the data set (Al-Saraireh and Masarweh 2022). The detection mechanism involves:
1. data collection
2. implementation of data preprocessing
3. feature extraction and feature selection implementation
4. splitting the data into training and testing portions
5. model building and evaluation.

**Using machine learning**

A life cycle model for APT, in five stages, is proposed by Quintero-Bonilla and Martín del Rey (Quintero-Bonilla and Martín del Rey 2020), where in each stage the most frequently used TTPs associated, according to MITRE, were included (Swisscom 2019). APT has been divided into passive (that do not change data - ex: port scanning) and active (that change data - ex: DDoS attacks) actions, including from social engineering attacks to specific attacks such as unauthorized access to servers. Machine learning (ML) is used by potential targets to analyze large amounts of data, such as IDS alerts, logs, or unauthorized remote connections; to identify any abnormal network behavior associated with an APT attack.

For APT detection based on the APT life cycle, Quintero-Bonilla and Martín del Rey propose the following steps (Quintero-Bonilla and Martín del Rey 2020):

- *Target discovery*: Passive network exploration where the attacker can perform port scanning techniques (e.g. Nmap tools), search for indexed services on the Internet (web surveillance cameras, servers or SCADA systems, with tools such as Shodan), public profiles in employee social networks and OSINT reconnaissance tools (e.g., spider leg).
    - o For *protection*, it is recommended to close unused ports, use firewalls, IDS, and secure virtual private connections (VLANs and VPNs), create password policies and know the user organization.
- *Exploitation*: Gaining network access through detected vulnerabilities, using techniques such as spear-phishing for valid accounts or USB replication. The attacker exploits the detected vulnerability using scripting, powershell and user execution, then remote management to establish a connection to the target network.
    - o As a *protection*, avoid using personal devices on the network and opening suspicious files. ML techniques allow the creation of automated solutions, for example a module that scans emails for malicious links or files. Or it can use network traffic scanning for unauthorized remote connections, log analysis for activity, or anomalous software updates. Implementing ML solutions requires a training dataset in the normal flow of the organization and another dataset with anomalous network flow. Tests must be performed in a controlled environment. The best performing ML algorithms were k-NN and SVM.

- *Internal intrusion*: After compromising the host, the attacker escalates privileges to access information of interest, this is the longest stage. Persistence is done through redundant access, account manipulation, or a web shell. Access to credentials can be gained through brute force techniques, account manipulation, forced authentication, or removal of credentials. Avoiding defense systems (IDS, IPS, firewall) can be done through proxy connections and hiding files or information.
    - As *protection* solutions are ML techniques for analyzing logs generated by IDS/IPS to detect possible APT attack patterns (unsuccessful access to SSH, FTP or telnet services), analysis of system logs (unauthorized program installations, directories, and files with code names, unknown hosts on the network). ML algorithms such as k-means, NB and SVM can be used.
- *Setting up data exfiltration channels*: establishing a connection with the C&C server to send the information, usually compressed and encrypted, and limiting the size of the packets. The attacker can use fast-flow techniques for connections, with data initially collected at one place in an area of the network and transmitted in small packets at different times. Data extraction can be automated and performed on different media using domain generation protocols, remote access tools, and multi-layer encryption.
    - Data exfiltration *detection* can use ML techniques to look for hosts with encrypted data, connections with random IP addresses and DNS, and encrypted data flows to unknown and unauthorized servers. k-NN and k-means algorithms can be used for APT detection.
- *Trace deletion*: After completing the mission, the attacker removes network attack traces from compromised systems (logs, compressed files, installed software or malware). If the attacker has reached this stage, in principle the victim will no longer know that he has been attacked.

Every organization must include in its cyber security plan the security policies adapted to its infrastructure. Identifying possible attacks in stages makes it easier to detect APTs, helping to anticipate these anomalous behaviors in the network.

# PROACTIVE DEFENSE STRATEGIES

APT detection requires a proactive defense posture. This section presents strategies such as continuous monitoring, penetration testing, and teaming to identify vulnerabilities before threat actors can exploit them. It also highlights the importance of employee training and awareness programs to mitigate the human factor in APT attacks.

Some new approaches mainly focus on early detection to limit long-term negative effects (Brewer 2014), a major challenge in securing complex critical systems.

Proactive protection allows identifying and securing an attack point before vulnerabilities are exploited by protecting them, using anti-virus software and blacklisting, scanning and behavioral analysis. Communication protocol scanning enables advanced detection of potential intruders. Protection must be long-term and persistent.

Organizational awareness and information technology education are the most important measures to proactively mitigate organizational cyber security threats. Administrators must learn how to effectively use emerging technology so that it provides additional protection (M. Cobb 2013). In the case of " cybercriminals, such as zero-day vulnerabilities and denial of service (DoS) attacks, conventional solutions cannot cope with the current complexity of these types of threats" (Quintero-Bonilla and Martín del Rey 2020). Furthermore, Quintero and Martin state that "Cybersecurity is responsible for establishing security policies; these policies set out the steps to follow for data to be managed within the technological infrastructure in an organisation. However, some security flaws and vulnerabilities (e.g., the use of outdated equipment, use of policies that are not reviewed continuously, failing to install updates at time, awareness deficiency) allow attackers to realise an intrusion in an organization." (Quintero-Bonilla and Martín del Rey 2020). Radzikowski recommends that advance incident response planning can significantly improve the organizational chances of early detection and more effective remediation (Radzikowski 2015). The key to effective protection, detection and response against APTs is a rigorous implementation of security best practices and ongoing education with the most targeted users. On the other hand, Hejase and Hejase emphasize that the government, businesses and educational institutions should join efforts to at least start an awareness campaign for everyone to introduce the terms of cyber warfare, cyber-attacks, cyber security and cyber weapons in the dictionary of everyday words, simply because the threat of a cyber-attack is ever-present and will not go away (A. Hejase, Hejase, and Hejase 2015, 87).

Chu, Lin, and Chang propose an early detection system for APT attacks, using the NSL-KDD database for attack detection and verification (Chu, Lin, and Chang 2019). The used method is principal component analysis

(PCA) to sample features and improve detection efficiency. The classifiers are then compared to detect the dataset; the classifier supports vector machine, naive bayes classification, decision tree and neural networks. Chu, Lin, and Chang conclude that support vector machine (SVM) has the highest recognition rate.

Many previous experiments have been performed using the KDD 99 database (McHugh 2000), which is based on a database established by DARPA in 1999 at Lincoln Labs at the Massachusetts Institute of Technology (MIT). It contains 494,021 records in the database training set and 311,029 records in the test set, with a total of 41 features and 5 types of large labels (normal, dos, r2l, u2l, samples). Tavallaee et al. modified the data sample by introducing the NSL-KDD database, which is more discriminative and allows better detection of intrusions (Tavallaee et al. 2009). The focus in this study was on exploring linear principal component analysis (PCA) (Bro and Smilde 2014) as the main axis. The NSL-KDD dataset was used for network intrusion detection. APT attack detection technology has also been combined with data mining techniques (Wu et al. 2008). The goal was to perform data integration and classification using sets of commonly encountered patterns and association rules to detect and obtain early warning of an APT attack.

To establish security countermeasures and procedures for a robust defense, Virvilis, Gritzalis, and Apostolopoulos created a specific environment based on which he established a set of recommendations, as follows (Virvilis, Gritzalis, and Apostolopoulos 2013):

- *Patch management*: For all network applications, being the first line of defense.
- *Network segregation*: Network controls and monitoring.
- *Whitelist*: Strict Internet access policies and granular traffic inspection with user restrictions.
- *Dynamic content execution*: Use of filtering mechanisms at network entry points.
- *A trusted computing system*: Limiting and controlling the software that can be installed and executed.

Hofer-Schmitz, Kleb, and Stojanović investigate the influences of different sets of statistical network traffic characteristics on advanced persistent threat detection using a semi-synthetic dataset, combining the CICIDS2017 dataset and the Contagio malware dataset (Hofer-Schmitz, Kleb, and Stojanović 2021). The obtained results showed a large impact of the choice of the feature set on the detection of APT signs, and an influence of the background data on the detection capabilities. The main conclusion was that investigating the features in more detail and building optimized and customized detection solutions can lead to saving processing resources and increasing detection performance.

Wang et al. relied on big data analysis and cloud computing technology to study the implementation of gene concept in networks attacked by APT (Y. Wang et al. 2014). Using the inverse analysis of network protocol and network data flow processing technology, a set of basic theories and technical architecture of network gene construction and computation is established, proposing a new detection framework for APT. The study considers the model of Oehmen et al. (Oehmen, Peterson, and Dowson 2010) based on the similarity between cybernetic entities and the behavior of organic systems for mapping the sequence of behaviors in the network. The network gene is defined as representing "the digital segments, extracted by network protocol reverse analysis, and their combined sequences that represent semantic-rich network behavior patterns of the network application. The subject of network gene is the network application (software)." (Y. Wang et al. 2016) The behavior models of a network application consists of three-level genes, such as message behavior gene, protocol behavior gene, and operational behavior gene from small to large, included in the Network Genome. Network gene-based APT monitoring is divided into two phases: automatic analysis and network gene extraction, and in-depth analysis of network abnormal behaviors based on real-time network gene computation. Tight correlations between genes facilitate the detection of APT attacks.

The main methods used by researchers to detect APT attacks are (Hassannataj Joloudari et al. 2020):

- Detection models based on machine learning algorithms, including linear support vector machine (Chu, Lin, and Chang 2019).
- Detection models based on mathematical models, such as the hidden Markov model (Ghafir et al. 2019).
- Methods and approaches for automatic feature extraction using attack graph (M. Lee 2011).
- Techniques to reduce false detection, such as the Duqu tool (Bencsáth et al. 2012).
- Detection of all attack steps using tools such as SpuNge (Balduzzi, Ciangaglini, and McArdle 2013).

Hassannataj Joloudari et al. state that these methods cannot perform timely detection when attacks occur in real time, proposing machine learning methods (such as C5.0 decision tree), Bayesian network and deep learning on the NSL-KDD dataset as the most effective approaches for improving the detection accuracy and proposing a 6-layer deep learning model by automatically extracting and selecting features from the hidden layers of the neural network (Hassannataj Joloudari et al. 2020).

# RELATED WORKS

Ghafir et al. highlights some related works on APT detection (Ghafir et al. 2019):

Balduzzi, Ciangaglini, and McArdle (Balduzzi, Ciangaglini, and McArdle 2013): SPuNge, a host-based APT detector that monitors the traffic of every host on the network and analyzes malicious URLs. Malicious connections can be established by hosts through an Internet browser or through malware installed on the compromised machine. Then, all machines showing similar activity are grouped together and considered part of an APT campaign.

Sigholm and Bang (Sigholm and Bang 2013): uses the Data Leakage Prevention (DLP) algorithm to detect data exfiltration. The proposed methodology uses a DLP algorithm to monitor the network traffic and analyze the transferred data or consults the connections to detect any data leakage. Then, fingerprints are produced based on the attributes of the leaked information. It uses external cyber counterintelligence (CCI) sensors to track the location or path of leaked data.

Brogi and Tong (Brogi and Tong 2016): TerminAPtor traces the flow of information to correlate alerts generated within the APT campaign based on the similarity of alert attributes that may be generated by another IDS such as Snort.

Wang et al. (Xu Wang et al. 2016): describe an APT detector based on command and control (C&C) domain detection, proposing a new function called Independent Access. The methodology analyzes DNS records and applies the RIPPER classification algorithm to classify domains into C&C and legal domains.

Nissim et al. (Nissim et al. 2015): uses active learning to detect malicious PDF files by analyzing network connections, using whitelists, reputation systems, and antivirus signature repository.

Chandra Jadala, Narasimham, and Pasupuleti (Chandra Jadala, Narasimham, and Pasupuleti 2020): present a methodology for detecting the spear phishing technique used to introduce the point of entry (PoE) into the targeted system in an APT. It relies on mathematical and computational analysis to detect spam emails.

Brogi and Bernardino (Brogi and Bernardino 2019): focuses on HMM-based techniques to classify APT scenarios that are reconstructed by other alert correlation tools.

Shin et al. (Shin et al. 2013): A probabilistic approach to predict a network intrusion using a Markov chain to model network events.

Kholidy et al (Kholidy et al. 2014): use an HMM to propose an adaptive risk approach for MSA prediction in cloud systems.

# NOTES ON APT DETECTION

In complex networks, a recurring anomaly may not be detected by a single rule. Only by combining multiple rules in the model can the approach reliably detect the evaluated anomaly. While this behavior is sufficient to detect most anomalies, it causes a large workload for the administrator when performing root cause analysis. A smarter approach to generating event classes is needed. Lack of information about event class similarities leads to redundant assumptions that could overload the system model. However, a more intelligent approach to hypothesis generation is not possible without knowledge of relationships or a hierarchy between classes of events. Given a hierarchy of event classes, an improved hypothesis generation algorithm should be developed. One approach would be an algorithm that generates all possible rules in a limited sub-tree of similar event classes and allows only the most significant or stable hypothesis to become a rule (Friedberg et al. 2015).

Using widely accepted best practices/countermeasures would reduce the impact of malware used in APTs. Unfortunately, it appears that even in critical infrastructures, only a small subset of such protection mechanisms has been applied. Since traditional security solutions have repeatedly failed to address the APT problem and organizations are reluctant to adopt high maintenance solutions/countermeasures, more robust and transparent solutions must be sought. A reliable computing base can be a useful tool in addressing this multidimensional problem (Virvilis, Gritzalis, and Apostolopoulos 2013).

Traditional network monitoring is difficult to systematically deal with APT attacks against its unique unpredictability, deep stealth and serious harmfulness. To overcome this challenge, new concepts are required to describe network behavior patterns, taking advantage of the latest advances in the fields of protocol inverse analysis, cloud computing and big data processing with automatic analysis and extraction and real-time processing, forming new detection frames for APT (Y. Wang et al. 2014).

Since the nature of APT attack is permanent and persistent presence in the victim's system, early detection of this attack requires high accuracy and minimum FPR in the early stages. The deep learning model is one of the best solutions in terms of accuracy in detecting APT attacks on datasets. Deep learning can be considered the highest and best system in most areas of network security detection. Ideally it would be a combination of machine learning and deep learning methods implemented on datasets and network traffic flow. In addition, supervised and unsupervised deep learning methods can be used, such as recurrent neural networks and autoencoding neural networks, respectively (Hassannataj Joloudari et al. 2020).

According to Alshamrani et al. . (Alshamrani et al. 2019), one of the most critical aspects to ensure the effectiveness of APT attack detection solutions is evaluation. Since APT attacks can be quite complex and deeply buried in regular network traffic, it is quite difficult to comprehensively test and evaluate such systems during development to improve their effectiveness against new attack methods/vectors through continuous algorithmic improvements and before deployment to adjust configurations and adapt them to specific environments, for example to meet performance criteria. The evaluation of APT attack detection methodologies lacks datasets from realistic attack scenarios, and an easy performance evaluation and comparison is much more difficult than in other IT fields.

Most current APT detection solutions evaluate proposed methodologies using machine learning models that typically involve three major components: data collection, feature extraction, and testing. Data collection can be from a real or virtual fabricated network scenario (synthetic model). The real network scenario has advantages such as realistic test base; however, it has disadvantages such as poor scalability in terms of user input, varied scenarios, privacy issues, and an attack on one's own system is required. Using a synthetic model to create the data allows full control over the amount of data collected and how the network is configured.

Another important component is the feature selection, which is a major aspect that affects results when using machine learning to solve a problem. Typically, the data collected is raw data and cannot be used directly for evaluating machine learning models. Therefore, it is necessary to pre-process the raw data and then select the required features. Features selected from one APT detection solution are not required to be used in another solution. Usually, the formalization of the problem has an influence on this task and determines which features can be selected. A feature is information associated with a feature and/or behavior of the object, where the feature may be static (e.g., derived from metadata associated with the object) and/or dynamic (e.g., based on actions performed by the object after virtual processing of the object) (Alshamrani et al. 2019).

# CONCLUSION

In an era where cyber threats are continuously evolving, understanding and defending against APTs is crucial for organizations and nations. APTs are a persistent and formidable challenge, but with proactive security measures, international cooperation and the use of cutting-edge technologies, it is possible to improve cyber security and reduce the risk of APT-related incidents. As APTs continue to adapt and grow in sophistication, the fight against them will be ongoing, demanding vigilance and innovation from the cybersecurity community.

In conclusion, detection of advanced persistent threats requires a comprehensive and dynamic approach. Organizations must continually adapt their strategies, leverage technological advances, threat intelligence and proactive defenses to effectively identify and mitigate the risks posed by APTs. By understanding the evolving nature of APTs and implementing a multi-layered defense strategy, the cybersecurity community can better protect against these persistent threats.

Countries ended up spying on each other to improve their weaponry or just to find out what the other nations were developing in their governments and militaries. But how will the nations that are being spied on react when they discover that their data is being stolen? Will this be the breeding ground for a cyber war of nations, or has it already begun? Even if this war is being waged in cyberspace, who knows how and where it will end up, and the impact and implications of such a war?

# BIBLIOGRAPHY

Adams, Chris. 2018. "Learning the Lessons of WannaCry." *Computer Fraud & Security* 2018 (9): 6–9. https://doi.org/10.1016/S1361-3723(18)30084-8.

Adelaiye, Oluwasegun, Aminat Ajibola, and Faki Silas. 2019. "Evaluating Advanced Persistent Threats Mitigation Effects: A Review," February.

Aleroud, Ahmed, and Lina Zhou. 2017. "Phishing Environments, Techniques, and Countermeasures: A Survey." *Computers & Security* 68 (July):160–96. https://doi.org/10.1016/j.cose.2017.04.006.

Alperovitch, Dmitri. 2011. "Revealed: Operation Shady RAT - McAfee." https://icscsi.org/library/Documents/Cyber_Events/McAfee%20-%20Operation%20Shady%20RAT.pdf.

Al-Saraireh, Jaafer, and Ala' Masarweh. 2022. "A Novel Approach for Detecting Advanced Persistent Threats." *Egyptian Informatics Journal* 23 (4): 45–55. https://doi.org/10.1016/j.eij.2022.06.005.

Alshamrani, Adel, Sowmya Myneni, Ankur Chowdhary, and Dijiang Huang. 2019. "A Survey on Advanced Persistent Threats: Techniques, Solutions, Challenges, and Research Opportunities." *IEEE Communications Surveys & Tutorials* 21 (2): 1851–77. https://doi.org/10.1109/COMST.2019.2891891.

Al-Yaseen, Wathiq Laftah, Zulaiha Ali Othman, and Mohd Zakree Ahmad Nazri. 2017. "Multi-Level Hybrid Support Vector Machine and Extreme Learning Machine Based on Modified K-Means for Intrusion Detection System." *Expert Systems with Applications* 67 (January):296–303. https://doi.org/10.1016/j.eswa.2016.09.041.

Amouri, Amar, Vishwa T. Alaparthy, and Salvatore D. Morgera. 2020. "A Machine Learning Based Intrusion Detection System for Mobile Internet of Things." *Sensors* 20 (2): 461. https://doi.org/10.3390/s20020461.

Apruzzese, Giovanni, Fabio Pierazzi, Michele Colajanni, and Mirco Marchetti. 2017. "Detection and Threat Prioritization of Pivoting Attacks in Large Networks." *IEEE Transactions on Emerging Topics in Computing* PP (October):1–1. https://doi.org/10.1109/TETC.2017.2764885.

Arachchilage, Nalin, and Steve Love. 2014. "Security Awareness of Computer Users: A Phishing Threat Avoidance Perspective." *Computers in Human Behavior* 38 (September):304–12. https://doi.org/10.1016/j.chb.2014.05.046.

Arntz, Pieter. 2016. "Explained: Advanced Persistent Threat (APT) | Malwarebytes Labs." Malwarebytes. July 25, 2016. https://www.malwarebytes.com/blog/news/2016/07/explained-advanced-persistent-threat-apt/.

Ashford, Warwick. 2011. "How to Combat Advanced Persistent Threats: APT Strategies to Protect Your Organisation | Computer Weekly." ComputerWeekly.Com. 2011. https://www.computerweekly.com/feature/How-to-combat-advanced-persistent-threats-APT-strategies-to-protect-your-organisation.

Ask, M. 2013. "Advanced Persistent Threat ( APT ) Beyond the Hype Project Report in IMT 4582 Network Security at Gjøvik University College during Spring 2013." In . https://www.semanticscholar.org/paper/Advanced-Persistent-Threat-(-APT-)-Beyond-the-hype-Ask/a140cd962b136474685db82de60bb15f4fe1d7e1.

Axelsson, Stefan. 2000. "The Base-Rate Fallacy and the Difficulty of Intrusion Detection." *ACM Transactions on Information and System Security* 3 (3): 186–205. https://doi.org/10.1145/357830.357849.

Azaria, Amos, Ariella Richardson, Sarit Kraus, and V. Subrahmanian. 2014. "Behavioral Analysis of Insider Threat: A Survey and Bootstrapped Prediction in Imbalanced Data." *IEEE Transactions on Computational Social Systems* 1 (June):135–55. https://doi.org/10.1109/TCSS.2014.2377811.

Bai, Tim, Haibo Bian, Abbas Abou Daya, Mohammad Salahuddin, Noura Limam, and Raouf Boutaba. 2019. *A Machine Learning Approach for RDP-Based Lateral Movement Detection.* https://doi.org/10.1109/LCN44214.2019.8990853.

Balduzzi, Marco, Vincenzo Ciangaglini, and Robert McArdle. 2013. *Targeted Attacks Detection with SPuNge.* https://doi.org/10.1109/PST.2013.6596053.

BBC. 2009. "Major Cyber Spy Network Uncovered," March 29, 2009. http://news.bbc.co.uk/2/hi/americas/7970471.stm.

Bencsáth, B., Gábor Pék, L. Buttyán, and M. Félegyházi. 2012. "Duqu: Analysis, Detection, and Lessons Learned." In . https://www.semanticscholar.org/paper/Duqu%3A-Analysis%2C-Detection%2C-and-Lessons-Learned-Bencs%C3%A1th-P%C3%A9k/9974cdf65ffbdee47837574432b0f8b59ffbddd1.

Benjamin, Victor, Weifeng Li, and Thomas Holt. 2015. *Exploring Threats and Vulnerabilities in Hacker Web: Forums, IRC and Carding Shops.* https://doi.org/10.1109/ISI.2015.7165944.

Bere, Mercy, Fungai Bhunu Shava, Attlee Gamundani, and Isaac Nhamu. 2015. "How Advanced Persistent Threats Exploit Humans." *IJCSI*, November.

Bertino, Elisa, and Gabriel Ghinita. 2011. "Towards Mechanisms for Detection and Prevention of Data Exfiltration by Insiders: Keynote Talk Paper." In *Proceedings of the 6th ACM Symposium on Information, Computer and Communications Security,* 10–19. Hong Kong China: ACM. https://doi.org/10.1145/1966913.1966916.

Bhatt, Parth, Edgar Toshiro Yano, and Per Gustavsson. 2014. "Towards a Framework to Detect Multi-Stage Advanced Persistent Threats Attacks." In *2014 IEEE 8th International Symposium on Service Oriented System Engineering,* 390–95. https://doi.org/10.1109/SOSE.2014.53.

Bowen, Brian M., Shlomo Hershkop, Angelos D. Keromytis, and Salvatore J. Stolfo. 2009. "Baiting Inside Attackers Using Decoy Documents." In

*Security and Privacy in Communication Networks*, edited by Yan Chen, Tassos D. Dimitriou, and Jianying Zhou, 51–70. Lecture Notes of the Institute for Computer Sciences, Social Informatics and Telecommunications Engineering. Berlin, Heidelberg: Springer. https://doi.org/10.1007/978-3-642-05284-2_4.

Brewer, Ross. 2014. "Advanced Persistent Threats: Minimising the Damage." *Network Security* 2014 (April):5–9. https://doi.org/10.1016/S1353-4858(14)70040-6.

Bro, Rasmus, and Age K. Smilde. 2014. "Principal Component Analysis." *Analytical Methods* 6 (9): 2812–31. https://doi.org/10.1039/C3AY41907J.

Brogi, Guillaume, and Elena Di Bernardino. 2019. "Hidden Markov Models for Advanced Persistent Threats." *International Journal of Security and Networks* 14 (4): 181. https://doi.org/10.1504/IJSN.2019.103147.

Brogi, Guillaume, and Valerie Viet Triem Tong. 2016. "TerminAPTor: Highlighting Advanced Persistent Threats through Information Flow Tracking." *2016 8th IFIP International Conference on New Technologies, Mobility and Security (NTMS)*, November, 1–5. https://doi.org/10.1109/NTMS.2016.7792480.

Bulgurcu, Burcu, Hasan Cavusoglu, and Izak Benbasat. 2010. "Information Security Policy Compliance: An Empirical Study of Rationality-Based Beliefs and Information Security Awareness." *MIS Quarterly* 34 (3): 523–48. https://doi.org/10.2307/25750690.

Busby, J. S., B. S. S. Onggo, and Y. Liu. 2016. "Agent-Based Computational Modelling of Social Risk Responses." *European Journal of Operational Research* 251 (3): 1029–42. https://doi.org/10.1016/j.ejor.2015.12.034.

Chaitanya, Krishna T., HariGopal Ponnapalli, Dylan Herts, and Juan Pablo. 2012. "Analysis and Detection of Modern Spam Techniques on Social Networking Sites." *2012 Third International Conference on Services in Emerging Markets*, December, 147–52. https://doi.org/10.1109/ICSEM.2012.28.

Chandola, Varun, Arindam Banerjee, and Vipin Kumar. 2009. "Anomaly Detection: A Survey." *ACM Comput. Surv.* 41 (July). https://doi.org/10.1145/1541880.1541882.

Chandra Jadala, Dr, Challa Narasimham, and Sai Kiran Pasupuleti. 2020. "Detection of Deceptive Phishing Based on Machine Learning Techniques." In , 13–22. https://doi.org/10.1007/978-981-15-2407-3_2.

Chen, Ping, Lieven Desmet, and Christophe Huygens. 2014. "A Study on Advanced Persistent Threats." In *Communications and Multimedia Security*, edited by Bart De Decker and André Zúquete, 63–72. Lecture Notes in Computer Science. Berlin, Heidelberg: Springer. https://doi.org/10.1007/978-3-662-44885-4_5.

Chen, Zhiyan, Jinxin Liu, Yu Shen, Murat Simsek, Burak Kantarci, H.T. Mouftah, and Petar Djukic. 2022. "Machine Learning-Enabled IoT Security: Open Issues and Challenges Under Advanced Persistent Threats." *ACM Computing Surveys* 55 (April). https://doi.org/10.1145/3530812.

Chu, Wen-Lin, Chih-Jer Lin, and Ke-Neng Chang. 2019. "Detection and Classification of Advanced Persistent Threats and Attacks Using the

Support Vector Machine." *Applied Sciences* 9 (21): 4579. https://doi.org/10.3390/app9214579.

Cisco. 2023. "What Is an Advanced Persistent Threat (APT)?" Cisco. 2023. https://www.cisco.com/c/en/us/products/security/advanced-persistent-threat.html.

CloudStrike. 2023. "Cyber Attacks on SMBs: Current Stats and How to Prevent Them." Crowdstrike.Com. 2023. https://www.crowdstrike.com/solutions/small-business/cyber-attacks-on-smbs/.

Cobb, Michael. 2013. "The Evolution of Threat Detection and Management." https://docs.media.bitpipe.com/io_10x/io_109837/item_691345/EMC_sSecurity_IO%23109837_E-Guide_060513.pdf.

Cobb, Stephen. 1996. *The NCSA Guide to PC and LAN Security*. McGraw-Hill.

Cole, Eric. 2013. *Advanced Persistent Threat: Understanding the Danger and How to Protect Your Organization*. Syngress.

Conti, Mauro, Luigi V. Mancini, Riccardo Spolaor, and Nino Vincenzo Verde. 2015. "Can't You Hear Me Knocking: Identification of User Actions on Android Apps via Traffic Analysis." In *Proceedings of the 5th ACM Conference on Data and Application Security and Privacy*, 297–304. CODASPY '15. New York, NY, USA: Association for Computing Machinery. https://doi.org/10.1145/2699026.2699119.

Coppolino, L., Michael Jäger, Nicolai Kuntze, and Roland Rieke. 2012. "A Trusted Information Agent for Security Information and Event Management." In , 6–12.

Crouse, Michael, Bryan Prosser, and Errin Fulp. 2015. *Probabilistic Performance Analysis of Moving Target and Deception Reconnaissance Defenses*. https://doi.org/10.1145/2808475.2808480.

CSS. 2019. "Trend Analysis - The Israeli Unit 8200 An OSINT-Based Study." CSS CYBER DEFENSE PROJECT. https://css.ethz.ch/content/dam/ethz/special-interest/gess/cis/center-for-securities-studies/pdfs/Cyber-Reports-2019-12-Unit-8200.pdf.

Daly, Michael K. 2009. "The Advanced Persistent Threat (or Informa5onized Force Opera5ons)." https://www.usenix.org/legacy/event/lisa09/tech/slides/daly.pdf.

De Vries, Johannes, Hans Hoogstraaten, Jan Van Den Berg, and Semir Daskapan. 2012. "Systems for Detecting Advanced Persistent Threats: A Development Roadmap Using Intelligent Data Analysis." *2012 International Conference on Cyber Security*, December, 54–61. https://doi.org/10.1109/CyberSecurity.2012.14.

Deloitte. 2016. "Cyber Espionage - The Harsh Reality of Advanced Security Threats." https://indianstrategicknowledgeonline.com/web/us_aers_cyber_espionage_07292011.pdf.

Denault, Michel, Dimitris Karagiannis, Dimitris Gritzalis, and Paul Spirakis. 1994. "Intrusion Detection: Approach and Performance Issues of the SECURENET System." *Computers & Security* 13 (6): 495–508. https://doi.org/10.1016/0167-4048(91)90138-4.

Denning, D.E. 1987. "An Intrusion-Detection Model." *IEEE Transactions on Software Engineering* SE-13 (2): 222–32. https://doi.org/10.1109/TSE.1987.232894.

Dijk, Marten van, Ari Juels, Alina Oprea, and Ronald L. Rivest. 2013. "FlipIt: The Game of 'Stealthy Takeover.'" *Journal of Cryptology* 26 (4): 655–713. https://doi.org/10.1007/s00145-012-9134-5.

EC-Council. 2023. "What Is Cyber Threat Modeling | Importance of Threat Modeling." *EC-Council* (blog). 2023. https://www.eccouncil.org/threat-modeling/.

Edwards, Benjamin, Tyler Moore, George Stelle, Steven Hofmeyr, and Stephanie Forrest. 2012. "Beyond the Blacklist: Modeling Malware Spread and the Effect of Interventions." *Proceedings New Security Paradigms Workshop*, February. https://doi.org/10.1145/2413296.2413302.

Eke, Hope Nkiruka, Andrei Petrovski, and Hatem Ahriz. 2019. "The Use of Machine Learning Algorithms for Detecting Advanced Persistent Threats." In *Proceedings of the 12th International Conference on Security of Information and Networks*, 1–8. SIN '19. New York, NY, USA: Association for Computing Machinery. https://doi.org/10.1145/3357613.3357618.

ETDA. 2023. "Threat Group Cards: A Threat Actor Encyclopedia." 2023. https://apt.etda.or.th/cgi-bin/aptgroups.cgi.

Falliere, Nicolas, Liam O Murchu, and Eric Chien. 2011. "W32.Stuxnet Dossier." Symantec. https://www.wired.com/images_blogs/threatlevel/2011/02/Symantec-Stuxnet-Update-Feb-2011.pdf.

Feily, Maryam, Alireza Shahrestani, and Sureswaran Ramadass. 2009. "A Survey of Botnet and Botnet Detection." *2009 Third International Conference on Emerging Security Information, Systems and Technologies*, 268–73. https://doi.org/10.1109/SECURWARE.2009.48.

Ferrer, Zarestel, and Methusela Cebrian Ferrer. 2010. "In-Depth Analysis of Hydraq - The Face of Cyberwar Enemies Unfolds." http://cybercampaigns.net/wp-content/uploads/2013/05/Hydraq.pdf.

FireEye. 2019. "Cyber Threats to the Financial Services and Insurance Industries." https://web.archive.org/web/20190811091624/https://www.fireeye.com/content/dam/fireeye-www/solutions/pdfs/ib-finance.pdf.

Fortinet. 2023. "What Is a Watering Hole Attack?" Fortinet. 2023. https://www.fortinet.com/resources/cyberglossary/watering-hole-attack.

Friedberg, Ivo, and Roman Fiedler. 2014. "Dealing with Advanced Persistent Threats in Smart Grid ICT Networks: 5th IEEE Innovative Smart Grid Technologies Conference." Edited by Florian Skopik. *Proceedings of the 5th IEEE Innovative Smart Grid Technologies Conference*, 1–6.

Friedberg, Ivo, Florian Skopik, Giuseppe Settanni, and Roman Fiedler. 2015. "Combating Advanced Persistent Threats: From Network Event Correlation to Incident Detection." *Computers & Security* 48 (February):35–57. https://doi.org/10.1016/j.cose.2014.09.006.

García-Teodoro, Pedro, Jesús Díaz-Verdejo, Gabriel Maciá-Fernández, and Enrique Vázquez. 2009. "Anomaly-Based Network Intrusion Detection:

Techniques, Systems and Challenges." *Computers & Security* 28 (February):18–28. https://doi.org/10.1016/j.cose.2008.08.003.

Ghafir, Ibrahim, Mohammad Hammoudeh, Vaclav Prenosil, Liangxiu Han, Robert Hegarty, Khaled Rabie, and Francisco J. Aparicio-Navarro. 2018. "Detection of Advanced Persistent Threat Using Machine-Learning Correlation Analysis." *Future Generation Computer Systems* 89 (December):349–59. https://doi.org/10.1016/j.future.2018.06.055.

Ghafir, Ibrahim, Konstantinos Kyriakopoulos, Francisco Aparicio-Navarro, S. Lambotharan, Basil AsSadhan, and Hamad BinSalleeh. 2018. "A Basic Probability Assignment Methodology for Unsupervised Wireless Intrusion Detection." *IEEE Access* PP (July):40008–23. https://doi.org/10.1109/ACCESS.2018.2855078.

Ghafir, Ibrahim, Konstantinos G. Kyriakopoulos, Sangarapillai Lambotharan, Francisco J. Aparicio-Navarro, Basil Assadhan, Hamad Binsalleeh, and Diab M. Diab. 2019. "Hidden Markov Models and Alert Correlations for the Prediction of Advanced Persistent Threats." *IEEE Access* 7:99508–20. https://doi.org/10.1109/ACCESS.2019.2930200.

Ghafir, Ibrahim, and Vaclav Prenosil. 2014. "Advanced Persistent Threat Attack Detection: An Overview." *International Journal Of Advances In Computer Networks And Its Security*, December, 154.

———. 2016. "Proposed Approach for Targeted Attacks Detection." In *Advanced Computer and Communication Engineering Technology*, edited by Hamzah Asyrani Sulaiman, Mohd Azlishah Othman, Mohd Fairuz Iskandar Othman, Yahaya Abd Rahim, and Naim Che Pee, 73–80. Lecture Notes in Electrical Engineering. Cham: Springer International Publishing. https://doi.org/10.1007/978-3-319-24584-3_7.

Giura, P., and Wei Wang. 2012. "Using Large Scale Distributed Computing to Unveil Advanced Persistent Threats." *Science*. https://www.semanticscholar.org/paper/Using-Large-Scale-Distributed-Computing-to-Unveil-Giura-Wang/75e702d56a4a90f9c773a0e1fd0074cbe6910ead.

Giura, Paul, and Wei Wang. 2012. "A Context-Based Detection Framework for Advanced Persistent Threats." In *2012 International Conference on Cyber Security*, 69–74. https://doi.org/10.1109/CyberSecurity.2012.16.

Greitzer, Frank L., and Deborah A. Frincke. 2010. "Combining Traditional Cyber Security Audit Data with Psychosocial Data: Towards Predictive Modeling for Insider Threat Mitigation." In *Insider Threats in Cyber Security*, edited by Christian W. Probst, Jeffrey Hunker, Dieter Gollmann, and Matt Bishop, 85–113. Advances in Information Security. Boston, MA: Springer US. https://doi.org/10.1007/978-1-4419-7133-3_5.

Grow, Brian, Keith Epstein, and Chi-Chu Tschang. 2008. "The New E-Spionage Threat." *BusinessWeek*. https://web.archive.org/web/20110418080952/http://www.businessweek.com/magazine/content/08_16/b4080032218430.htm.

Gu, Guofei, Roberto Perdisci, Junjie Zhang, and Wenke Lee. 2008. *BotMiner: Clustering Analysis of Network Traffic for Protocol- and Structure-Independent Botnet Detection. CCS'08.*

Guerra-Manzanares, Alejandro, Sven Nõmm, and Hayretdin Bahsi. 2019. "Towards the Integration of a Post-Hoc Interpretation Step into the Machine Learning Workflow for IoT Botnet Detection." In *2019 18th IEEE International Conference On Machine Learning And Applications (ICMLA)*, 1162–69. https://doi.org/10.1109/ICMLA.2019.00193.

Gulati, Radha. 2003. "The Threat of Social Engineering and Your Defense Against It | SANS Institute." 2003. https://www.sans.org/white-papers/1232/.

Hachem, Nabil, Yosra Ben Mustapha, Gustavo Gonzalez Granadillo, and Herve Debar. 2011. "Botnets: Lifecycle and Taxonomy." In *2011 Conference on Network and Information Systems Security*, 1–8. https://doi.org/10.1109/SAR-SSI.2011.5931395.

Haddadpajouh, Hamed, Ali Dehghantanha, Raouf Khayami, and Kim-Kwang Raymond Choo. 2018. "A Deep Recurrent Neural Network Based Approach for Internet of Things Malware Threat Hunting." *Future Generation Computer Systems* 85 (March). https://doi.org/10.1016/j.future.2018.03.007.

Hamilton, S., W. L. Miller, Allen Ott, and O. S. Saydjari. 2002. "Challenges in Applying Game Theory to the Domain of Information Warfare †." In . https://www.semanticscholar.org/paper/Challenges-in-Applying-Game-Theory-to-the-Domain-of-Hamilton-Miller/a65d0d3c8aae0f35a524c84d15748f85b01df7de.

Hartigan, John A. 1975. *Clustering Algorithms*. Wiley.

Hasan, Mahmudul, Md Islam, Ishrak Islam, and M.M.A. Hashem. 2019. "Attack and Anomaly Detection in IoT Sensors in IoT Sites Using Machine Learning Approaches," May, 100059. https://doi.org/10.1016/j.iot.2019.100059.

Hassannataj Joloudari, Javad, Mojtaba Haderbadi, Amir Mashmool, Mohammad Ghasemigol, Shahab Shamshirband, and Amir Mosavi. 2020. "Early Detection of the Advanced Persistent Threat Attack Using Performance Analysis of Deep Learning." *IEEE Access* 8 (October). https://doi.org/10.1109/ACCESS.2020.3029202.

Hejase, Ale, Hussin Hejase, and Jose Hejase. 2015. "Cyber Warfare Awareness in Lebanon: Exploratory Research." *International Journal of Cyber-Security and Digital Forensics* Vol 4 (September):482–97. https://doi.org/10.17781/P001892.

Hejase, Hussin, Hasan Kazan, and Imad Moukadem. 2020. *Advanced Persistent Threats (APT): An Awareness Review*. https://doi.org/10.13140/RG.2.2.31300.65927.

Hinton, Geoffrey. 2009. "Deep Belief Networks." *Scholarpedia* 4 (January):5947. https://doi.org/10.4249/scholarpedia.5947.

Hochreiter, Sepp, and Jürgen Schmidhuber. 1997. "Long Short-Term Memory." *Neural Computation* 9 (December):1735–80. https://doi.org/10.1162/neco.1997.9.8.1735.

Hodge, Victoria J., and Jim Austin. 2004. "A Survey of Outlier Detection Methodologies." *Artificial Intelligence Review* 22 (2): 85–126. https://doi.org/10.1007/s10462-004-4304-y.

Hofer-Schmitz, Katharina, Ulrike Kleb, and Branka Stojanović. 2021. "The Influences of Feature Sets on the Detection of Advanced Persistent Threats." *Electronics* 10 (6): 704. https://doi.org/10.3390/electronics10060704.

Hofkirchner, Wolfgang, and Mark Burgin. 2017. *Future Information Society, The: Social And Technological Problems*. World Scientific.

Holland, Rick. 2013. "Introducing Forrester's Cyber Threat Intelligence Research." 2013. https://web.archive.org/web/20140415054512/http://blogs.forrester.co m/rick_holland/13-02-14-introducing_forresters_cyber_threat_intelligence_research.

Hudson, Barbara. 2013. "Advanced Persistent Threats: Detection, Protection and Prevention." https://i.crn.com/sites/default/files/ckfinderimages/userfiles/images/cr n/custom/Sophos_Advanced_Persistent_Threats.pdf.

Huh, Jun, John Lyle, Cornelius Namiluko, and Andrew Martin. 2011. "Managing Application Whitelists in Trusted Distributed Systems." *Future Generation Comp. Syst.* 27 (February):211–26. https://doi.org/10.1016/j.future.2010.08.014.

Hutchins, Eric, Michael Cloppert, and Rohan Amin. 2011. "Intelligence-Driven Computer Network Defense Informed by Analysis of Adversary Campaigns and Intrusion Kill Chains." *Leading Issues in Information Warfare & Security Research* 1 (January).

IC Espionage. 2010. "Shadows In The Cloud: Investigating Cyber Espionage 2.0." https://www.nartv.org/mirror/shadows-in-the-cloud.pdf.

ISACA. 2016. "Book Review: Advanced Persistent Threats." ISACA. 2016. https://www.isaca.org/resources/isaca-journal/issues/2016/volume-4/advanced-persistent-threats-how-to-manage-the-risk-to-your-business.

IT Governance. 2023. "Advanced Persistent Threats (APTs)." 2023. https://itgovernance.co.uk/advanced-persistent-threats-apt.

Jeun, Inkyung, Youngsook Lee, and Dongho Won. 2012. "A Practical Study on Advanced Persistent Threats." In *Computer Applications for Security, Control and System Engineering*, edited by Tai-hoon Kim, Adrian Stoica, Wai-chi Fang, Thanos Vasilakos, Javier García Villalba, Kirk P. Arnett, Muhammad Khurram Khan, and Byeong-Ho Kang, 144–52. Communications in Computer and Information Science. Berlin, Heidelberg: Springer. https://doi.org/10.1007/978-3-642-35264-5_21.

Jia, Bin, Zhaowen Lin, and Yan Ma. 2015. *Advanced Persistent Threat Detection Method Research Based on Relevant Algorithms to Artificial Immune System*. Vol. 520. https://doi.org/10.1007/978-3-662-47401-3_29.

Johnson, Ariana. 2016. "Cybersecurity for Financial Institutions: The Integral Role of Information Sharing in Cyber Attack Mitigation." *North Carolina Banking Institute* 20 (1): 277.

Johnson, John, and Emilie Hogan. 2013. *A Graph Analytic Metric for Mitigating Advanced Persistent Threat*. Vol. 129. https://doi.org/10.1109/ISI.2013.6578801.

Kaspersky. 2015. "The Duqu 2.0." https://media.kasperskycontenthub.com/wp-content/uploads/sites/43/2018/03/07205202/The_Mystery_of_Duqu_2_0_a_sophisticated_cyberespionage_actor_returns.pdf.

———. 2023a. "Targeted Cyberattacks Logbook." APT Kaspersky Securelist. 2023. https://apt.securelist.com.

———. 2023b. "What Is an Advanced Persistent Threat (APT)?" www.kaspersky.com. April 19, 2023. https://www.kaspersky.com/resource-center/definitions/advanced-persistent-threats.

Kaushik, Atul, Emmanuel Pilli, and R. Joshi. 2010. *Network Forensic System for Port Scanning Attack*. https://doi.org/10.1109/IADCC.2010.5422935.

Kholidy, Hisham A., Abdelkarim Erradi, Sherif Abdelwahed, and Abdulrahman Azab. 2014. "A Finite State Hidden Markov Model for Predicting Multistage Attacks in Cloud Systems." *2014 IEEE 12th International Conference on Dependable, Autonomic and Secure Computing*, August, 14–19. https://doi.org/10.1109/DASC.2014.12.

Kim, Hyunjoo, Jonghyun Kim, Ikkyun Kim, and Tai-myung Chung. 2015. "Behavior-Based Anomaly Detection on Big Data." *Australian Information Security Management Conference*, January. https://doi.org/10.4225/75/57b69d1ed938e.

Krombholz, Katharina, Heidelinde Hobel, Markus Huber, and Edgar Weippl. 2015. "Advanced Social Engineering Attacks." *Journal of Information Security and Applications*, Special Issue on Security of Information and Networks, 22 (June):113–22. https://doi.org/10.1016/j.jisa.2014.09.005.

Kyriakopoulos, Kostas, Francisco J. Aparicio-Navarro, Ibrahim Ghafir, Sangarapillai Lambotharan, and Jonathon Chambers. 2018. *Multi-stage attack detection using contextual information*. Loughborough University. https://doi.org/10.1109/MILCOM.2018.8599708'].

Langner, Ralph. 2011. "Stuxnet: Dissecting a Cyberwarfare Weapon." *IEEE Security & Privacy* 9 (3): 49–51. https://doi.org/10.1109/MSP.2011.67.

Lee, Bernard, Manmeet (Mandy) Mahinderjit Singh, and Azizul Rahman Mohd Shariff. 2019. "APTGuard : Advanced Persistent Threat (APT) Detections and Predictions Using Android Smartphone: 5th ICCST 2018, Kota Kinabalu, Malaysia, 29-30 August 2018." In , 545–55. https://doi.org/10.1007/978-981-13-2622-6_53.

Lee, Martin. 2011. "Clustering Disparate Attacks: Mapping The Activities of The Advanced Persistent Threat." *21st Virus Bulletin International Conference*, October. https://www.academia.edu/2352875/CLUSTERING_DISPARATE_ATTACKS_MAPPING_THE_ACTIVITIES_OF_THE_ADVANCED_PERSISTENT_THREAT.

Lemay, Antoine, Joan Calvet, François Menet, and José M. Fernandez. 2018. "Survey of Publicly Available Reports on Advanced Persistent Threat Actors." *Computers & Security* 72 (January):26–59. https://doi.org/10.1016/j.cose.2017.08.005.

Lim, Joo, Shanton Chang, Sean Maynard, and Atif Ahmad. 2009. "Exploring the Relationship between Organizational Culture and Information Security

Culture." *Australian Information Security Management Conference*, December. https://doi.org/10.4225/75/57b4065130def.

Lin, Min, Qiang Chen, and Shuicheng Yan. 2013. "Network In Network." *CoRR*, December. https://www.semanticscholar.org/paper/Network-In-Network-Lin-Chen/5e83ab70d0cbc003471e87ec306d27d9c80ecb16.

Liu, Yali, Cherita Corbett, Ken Chiang, Rennie Archibald, Biswanath Mukherjee, and Dipak Ghosal. 2009. *SIDD: A Framework for Detecting Sensitive Data Exfiltration by an Insider Attack. Hawaii International Conference on System Sciences.* https://doi.org/10.1109/HICSS.2009.390.

Lo, Chi-Chun, and Wan-Jia Chen. 2012. "A Hybrid Information Security Risk Assessment Procedure Considering Interdependences between Controls." *Expert Systems with Applications* 39 (1): 247–57. https://doi.org/10.1016/j.eswa.2011.07.015.

Lockheed Martin. 2023. "Cyber Kill Chain®." Lockheed Martin. 2023. https://www.lockheedmartin.com/en-us/capabilities/cyber/cyber-kill-chain.html.

Mahadevan, Vijay, Wei-Xin LI, Viral Bhalodia, and Nuno Vasconcelos. 2010. *Anomaly Detection in Crowded Scenes. Proceedings of the IEEE Computer Society Conference on Computer Vision and Pattern Recognition.* https://doi.org/10.1109/CVPR.2010.5539872.

Maloney, Sarah. 2018. "What Is an Advanced Persistent Threat (APT)?" 2018. https://www.cybereason.com/blog/advanced-persistent-threat-apt.

Mandiant. 2013. "APT1 | Exposing One of China's Cyber Espionage Units." Mandiant. 2013. https://www.mandiant.com/resources/reports/apt1-exposing-one-chinas-cyber-espionage-units.

———. 2021. "Today's Top Cyber Trends & Attacks Insights | M-Trends 2021." Mandiant. 2021. https://www.mandiant.com/resources/reports/m-trends-2021.

Manhas, Jatinder, and Shallu Kotwal. 2021. "Implementation of Intrusion Detection System for Internet of Things Using Machine Learning Techniques." In , edited by Kaiser J. Giri, Shabir Ahmad Parah, Rumaan Bashir, and Khan Muhammad, 217–37. Algorithms for Intelligent Systems. Singapore: Springer Singapore. https://doi.org/10.1007/978-981-15-8711-5_11.

Marchetti, Mirco, Fabio Pierazzi, Michele Colajanni, and Alessandro Guido. 2016. "Analysis of High Volumes of Network Traffic for Advanced Persistent Threat Detection." *Computer Networks* 109 (June). https://doi.org/10.1016/j.comnet.2016.05.018.

Matthews, Tim. 2019. "Operation Aurora – 2010's Major Breach by Chinese Hackers." Exabeam. January 8, 2019. https://www.exabeam.com/information-security/operation-aurora/.

McAfee. 2010a. "Protecting Your Critical Assets." https://www.wired.com/images_blogs/threatlevel/2010/03/operationaurora_wp_0310_fnl.pdf.

———. 2010b. "Protecting Your Critical Assets - Lessons Learned from 'Operation Aurora.'"

https://www.wired.com/images_blogs/threatlevel/2010/03/operationau rora_wp_0310_fnl.pdf.

———. 2018. "The Economic Impact of Cybercrime No Slowing Down." https://csis-website-prod.s3.amazonaws.com/s3fs-public/publication/economic-impact-cybercrime.pdf.

McDermott, Christopher D., Farzan Majdani, and Andrei V. Petrovski. 2018. "Botnet Detection in the Internet of Things Using Deep Learning Approaches." In *2018 International Joint Conference on Neural Networks (IJCNN)*, 1–8. https://doi.org/10.1109/IJCNN.2018.8489489.

McHugh, John. 2000. "Testing Intrusion Detection Systems: A Critique of the 1998 and 1999 DARPA Intrusion Detection System Evaluations as Performed by Lincoln Laboratory." *ACM Transactions on Information and System Security* 3 (4): 262–94. https://doi.org/10.1145/382912.382923.

McMahon, Dave, and Rafal Rohozinski. 2013. "The Dark Space Project: Defence R&D Canada – Centre for Security Science Contractor Report DRDC CSS CR 2013-007."

Merz, Terry. 2019. "A Context-Centred Research Approach to Phishing and Operational Technology in Industrial Control Systems | Journal of Information Warfare." 2019. https://www.jinfowar.com/journal/volume-18-issue-4/context-centred-research-approach-phishing-operational-technology-industrial-control-systems.

Messier, Ric. 2013. *GSEC GIAC Security Essentials Certification All-in-One Exam Guide*. McGraw Hill Professional.

Microsoft. 2022. "Threats - Microsoft Threat Modeling Tool - Azure - STRIDE." August 25, 2022. https://learn.microsoft.com/en-us/azure/security/develop/threat-modeling-tool-threats.

Milajerdi, Sadegh M., Rigel Gjomemo, Birhanu Eshete, R. Sekar, and V.N. Venkatakrishnan. 2019. "HOLMES: Real-Time APT Detection through Correlation of Suspicious Information Flows." In *2019 IEEE Symposium on Security and Privacy (SP)*, 1137–52. https://doi.org/10.1109/SP.2019.00026.

Mitnick, Kevin D., and William L. Simon. 2011. *The Art of Deception: Controlling the Human Element of Security*. John Wiley & Sons.

MITRE. 2021. "MiniDuke, Software S0051 | MITRE ATT&CK®." 2021. https://attack.mitre.org/software/S0051/.

Montgomery, Douglas C., Elizabeth A. Peck, and G. Geoffrey Vining. 2012. *Introduction to Linear Regression Analysis*. John Wiley & Sons.

Moon, Daesung, Hyungjin Im, Jae Dong Lee, and Jong Hyuk Park. 2014. "MLDS: Multi-Layer Defense System for Preventing Advanced Persistent Threats." *Symmetry* 6 (4): 997–1010. https://doi.org/10.3390/sym6040997.

Muszyński, Józef, and Greg Shipley. 2008. "Narzędzia SIEM (Security Information and Event Management)." Computerworld. 2008. https://www.computerworld.pl/news/Narzedzia-SIEM-Security-Information-and-Event-Management,325855.html.

Nance, Kara, and Matt Bishop. 2017. *Introduction to Deception, Digital Forensics, and Malware Minitrack*. https://doi.org/10.24251/HICSS.2017.731.

Nar, Kamil, and S. Shankar Sastry. 2018. "An Analytical Framework to Address the Data Exfiltration of Advanced Persistent Threats." In *2018 IEEE Conference on Decision and Control (CDC)*, 867–73. https://doi.org/10.1109/CDC.2018.8619834.

Nicho, Mathew, and Christopher D. McDermott. 2019. "Dimensions of 'Socio' Vulnerabilities of Advanced Persistent Threats." In *2019 International Conference on Software, Telecommunications and Computer Networks (SoftCOM)*, 1–5. https://doi.org/10.23919/SOFTCOM.2019.8903788.

Nick. 2018. "Turla APT Group's Espionage Campaigns Now Employs Adobe Flash Installer and Ingenious Social Engineering." *Cyber Defense Magazine* (blog). January 16, 2018. https://www.cyberdefensemagazine.com/turla-apt-groups-espionage-campaigns-now-employs-adobe-flash-installer-and-ingenious-social-engineering/.

Nissim, Nir, Aviad Cohen, Chanan Glezer, and Yuval Elovici. 2015. "Detection of Malicious PDF Files and Directions for Enhancements: A State-of-the Art Survey." *Computers & Security* 48 (February):246–66. https://doi.org/10.1016/j.cose.2014.10.014.

NIST, Initiative Joint Task Force Transformation. 2011. "Managing Information Security Risk: Organization, Mission, and Information System View." NIST Special Publication (SP) 800-39. National Institute of Standards and Technology. https://doi.org/10.6028/NIST.SP.800-39.

Nunes, Eric, Ahmad Diab, Andrew Gunn, Ericsson Marin, Vineet Mishra, Vivin Paliath, John Robertson, Jana Shakarian, Amanda Thart, and Paulo Shakarian. 2016. *Darknet and Deepnet Mining for Proactive Cybersecurity Threat Intelligence.* https://doi.org/10.1109/ISI.2016.7745435.

Oehmen, Christopher, Elena Peterson, and Scott Dowson. 2010. "An Organic Model for Detecting Cyber-Events." In *Proceedings of the Sixth Annual Workshop on Cyber Security and Information Intelligence Research*, 1–4. CSIIRW '10. New York, NY, USA: Association for Computing Machinery. https://doi.org/10.1145/1852666.1852740.

Paganini, Pierluigi. 2019. "Iran-Linked APT33 Updates Infrastructure Following Its Public Disclosure." Security Affairs. July 1, 2019. https://securityaffairs.com/87784/apt/apt33-updates-infrastructure.html.

Park, Seong-Taek, Guozhong Li, and Jae-Chang Hong. 2020. "A Study on Smart Factory-Based Ambient Intelligence Context-Aware Intrusion Detection System Using Machine Learning." *Journal of Ambient Intelligence and Humanized Computing* 11 (4): 1405–12. https://doi.org/10.1007/s12652-018-0998-6.

Parrish, Jr, James L., Janet L. Bailey, and James F. Courtney. 2009. "A Personality Based Model for Determining Susceptibility to Phishing Attacks." http://www.swdsi.org/swdsi2009/papers/9J05.pdf.

Peikert, Chris. 2016. "A Decade of Lattice Cryptography." *Foundations and Trends®️ in Theoretical Computer Science* 10 (4): 283–424. https://doi.org/10.1561/0400000074.

Pfleeger, Shari, Angela Sasse, and Adrian Furnham. 2014. "From Weakest Link to Security Hero: Transforming Staff Security Behavior." *Journal of Homeland*

*Security and Emergency Management* 11 (December). https://doi.org/10.1515/jhsem-2014-0035.

Probst, Philipp, Marvin N. Wright, and Anne-Laure Boulesteix. 2019. "Hyperparameters and Tuning Strategies for Random Forest." *WIREs Data Mining and Knowledge Discovery* 9 (3): e1301. https://doi.org/10.1002/widm.1301.

PWC. 2014. "Managing Cyber Risks in an Interconnected World." https://www.pwc.com/gx/en/consulting-services/information-security-survey/assets/the-global-state-of-information-security-survey-2015.pdf.

Quintero-Bonilla, Santiago, and Angel Martín del Rey. 2020. "A New Proposal on the Advanced Persistent Threat: A Survey." *Applied Sciences* 10 (11): 3874. https://doi.org/10.3390/app10113874.

Rachmadi, Salman, Satria Mandala, and Dita Oktaria. 2021. "Detection of DoS Attack Using AdaBoost Algorithm on IoT System." In *2021 International Conference on Data Science and Its Applications (ICoDSA)*, 28–33. https://doi.org/10.1109/ICoDSA53588.2021.9617545.

Radzikowski, Shem. 2015. "CyberSecurity: Origins of the Advanced Persistent Threat (APT)." Dr.Shem. October 8, 2015. https://DrShem.com/2015/10/08/cybersecurity-origins-of-the-advanced-persistent-threat-apt/.

Rafique, M. Zubair, Ping Chen, Christophe Huygens, and Wouter Joosen. 2014. "Evolutionary Algorithms for Classification of Malware Families through Different Network Behaviors." In *Proceedings of the 2014 Annual Conference on Genetic and Evolutionary Computation*, 1167–74. GECCO '14. New York, NY, USA: Association for Computing Machinery. https://doi.org/10.1145/2576768.2598238.

Rass, Stefan, Sandra König, and Stefan Schauer. 2017. "Defending Against Advanced Persistent Threats Using Game-Theory." *PLOS ONE* 12 (1): e0168675. https://doi.org/10.1371/journal.pone.0168675.

Roldán, José, Juan Boubeta-Puig, José Luis Martínez, and Guadalupe Ortiz. 2020. "Integrating Complex Event Processing and Machine Learning: An Intelligent Architecture for Detecting IoT Security Attacks." *Expert Systems with Applications* 149 (July):113251. https://doi.org/10.1016/j.eswa.2020.113251.

Rot, Artur. 2009. "Enterprise Information Technology Security: Risk Management Perspective." *Lecture Notes in Engineering and Computer Science* 2179 (October).

———. 2016. "Zarządzanie Ryzykiem w Cyberprzestrzeni – Wybrane Zagadnienia Teorii i Praktyki." In , 35–50.

Rot, Artur, and Bogusław Olszewski. 2017. *Advanced Persistent Threats Attacks in Cyberspace. Threats, Vulnerabilities, Methods of Protection.* https://doi.org/10.15439/2017F488.

Rowe, Mark. 2013. "Advanced Persistent Threats: How to Manage the Risk to Your Business." Professional Security. October 11, 2013. https://professionalsecurity.co.uk/reviews/advanced-persistent-threats-how-to-manage-the-risk-to-your-business/.

Russell, Chelsa. 2002. "Security Awareness - Implementing an Effective Strategy | SANS Institute." 2002. https://www.sans.org/white-papers/418/.

SANS. 2013. "Assessing Outbound Traffic to Uncover Advanced Persistent Threat." SANS Technology Institute.

Santoro, Diego, Gines Escudero-Andreu, Kostas Kyriakopoulos, Francisco J. Aparicio-Navarro, David J. Parish, and M. Vadursi. 2017. "A hybrid intrusion detection system for virtual jamming attacks on wireless networks," January, 79–87. https://doi.org/10.1016/j.measurement.2017.05.034'].

Sasaki, Takayuki. 2011. "Towards Detecting Suspicious Insiders by Triggering Digital Data Sealing." In *2011 Third International Conference on Intelligent Networking and Collaborative Systems*, 637–42. Fukuoka, Japan: IEEE. https://doi.org/10.1109/INCoS.2011.157.

Schatz, Daniel, Rabih Bashroush, and Julie Wall. 2017. "Towards a More Representative Definition of Cyber Security." *Journal of Digital Forensics, Security and Law* 12 (2). https://doi.org/10.15394/jdfsl.2017.1476.

Schmid, M., F. Hill, and A.K. Ghosh. 2002. "Protecting Data from Malicious Software." *18th Annual Computer Security Applications Conference, 2002. Proceedings.*, 199–208. https://doi.org/10.1109/CSAC.2002.1176291.

Schubert, Erich, Jörg Sander, Martin Ester, Hans Kriegel, and Xiaowei Xu. 2017. "DBSCAN Revisited, Revisited: Why and How You Should (Still) Use DBSCAN." *ACM Transactions on Database Systems* 42 (July):1–21. https://doi.org/10.1145/3068335.

SecureList. 2013. "'Red October' Diplomatic Cyber Attacks Investigation." January 14, 2013. https://securelist.com/red-october-diplomatic-cyber-attacks-investigation/36740/.

Sexton, Joseph, Curtis Storlie, and Joshua Neil. 2015. "Attack Chain Detection." *Statistical Analysis and Data Mining: The ASA Data Science Journal* 8 (5–6): 353–63. https://doi.org/10.1002/sam.11296.

Shalaginov, Andrii, Katrin Franke, and Xiongwei Huang. 2016. *Malware Beaconing Detection by Mining Large-Scale DNS Logs for Targeted Attack Identification.*

Shamah, David. n.d. "Cyber Espionage Bug Attacking Middle East, but Israel Untouched — so Far." Accessed December 12, 2023. http://www.timesofisrael.com/new-cyber-bug-targeting-middle-east-but-israel-untouched-so-far/.

Sharma, Pradip Kumar, Seo Yeon Moon, Daesung Moon, and Jong Hyuk Park. 2017. "DFA-AD: A Distributed Framework Architecture for the Detection of Advanced Persistent Threats." *Cluster Computing* 20 (1): 597–609. https://doi.org/10.1007/s10586-016-0716-0.

Shenwen, Lin, Li Yingbo, and Du Xiongjie. 2015. "Study and Research of APT Detection Technology Based on Big Data Processing Architecture." *2015 IEEE 5th International Conference on Electronics Information and Emergency Communication,* May, 313–16. https://doi.org/10.1109/ICEIEC.2015.7284547.

Shevchenko, Nataliya, Timothy A. Chick, Paige O'Riordan, and Thomas Patrick Scanlon. 2018. "Threat Modeling: A Summary of Available Methods." https://apps.dtic.mil/sti/citations/AD1084024.

Shin, Seongjun, Seungmin Lee, Hyunwoo Kim, and Sehun Kim. 2013. "Advanced Probabilistic Approach for Network Intrusion Forecasting and Detection." *Expert Systems with Applications* 40 (January):315–22. https://doi.org/10.1016/j.eswa.2012.07.057.

Shirey, Rob. 2000. "Internet Security Glossary." Request for Comments RFC 2828. Internet Engineering Task Force. https://doi.org/10.17487/RFC2828.

Siddiqui, Sana, Salman Khan, K. Ferens, and Witold Kinsner. 2016. *Detecting Advanced Persistent Threats Using Fractal Dimension Based Machine Learning Classification.* https://doi.org/10.1145/2875475.2875484.

Sigholm, Johan, and Martin Bang. 2013. *Towards Offensive Cyber Counterintelligence: Adopting a Target-Centric View on Advanced Persistent Threats.* https://doi.org/10.1109/EISIC.2013.37.

SignalSense. 2015. "Using Deep Learning To Detect Threat, SignalSense, White Paper,." https://www.ten-inc.com/presentations/deep_learning.pdf.

Sim, Kevin, Emma Hart, and Ben Paechter. 2014. "A Lifelong Learning Hyper-Heuristic Method for Bin Packing." *Evolutionary Computation* 23 (February). https://doi.org/10.1162/EVCO_a_00121.

Singer, Peter W., and Allan Friedman. 2014. *Cybersecurity: What Everyone Needs to Know.* OUP USA.

Singh, Abhishek, and Zheng Bu. 2014. "Hot Knives Through Butter: Bypassing Automated Analysis Systems (Black Hat USA 2013) - InfoconDB." 2014. https://infocondb.org/con/black-hat/black-hat-usa-2013/hot-knives-through-butter-bypassing-automated-analysis-systems.

Smart, Steven J. 2011. "Joint Targeting in Cyberspace." https://apps.dtic.mil/sti/citations/ADA555785.

Soong, T. T. 2004. "Fundamentals of Probability and Statistics for Engineers | Wiley." Wiley.Com. 2004. https://www.wiley.com/en-us/Fundamentals+of+Probability+and+Statistics+for+Engineers-p-9780470868157.

Sriram, S., R. Vinayakumar, Mamoun Alazab, and Soman KP. 2020. "Network Flow Based IoT Botnet Attack Detection Using Deep Learning." In *IEEE INFOCOM 2020 - IEEE Conference on Computer Communications Workshops (INFOCOM WKSHPS),* 189–94. https://doi.org/10.1109/INFOCOMWKSHPS50562.2020.9162668.

Stevens, Tim. 2018. "Global Cybersecurity: New Directions in Theory and Methods." *Politics and Governance* 6 (2): 1–4. https://doi.org/10.17645/pag.v6i2.1569.

Swisscom. 2019. "Report on the Threat Situation | SME | Swisscom." 2019. https://www.swisscom.ch/en/business/sme/downloads/report-threat-situation-switzerland-2019.html.

Symantec. 2018a. "2018 Internet Security Threat Report." https://docs.broadcom.com/doc/istr-23-executive-summary-en.

———. 2018b. "Advanced Persistent Threats: A Symantec Perspective." https://web.archive.org/web/20180508161501/https://www.symantec.com/content/en/us/enterprise/white_papers/b-advanced_persistent_threats_WP_21215957.en-us.pdf.

Taddeo, Mariarosaria. 2012. "An Analysis for a Just Cyber Warfare." In *2012 4th International Conference on Cyber Conflict (CYCON 2012)*, 1–10. https://ieeexplore.ieee.org/document/6243976.

Tanaka, Yasuyuki, Mitsuaki Akiyama, and Atsuhiro Goto. 2017. "Analysis of Malware Download Sites by Focusing on Time Series Variation of Malware." *Journal of Computational Science* 22 (September):301–13. https://doi.org/10.1016/j.jocs.2017.05.027.

Tankard, Colin. 2011. "Advanced Persistent Threats and How to Monitor and Deter Them." *Network Security* 2011 (8): 16–19. https://doi.org/10.1016/S1353-4858(11)70086-1.

Tavallaee, Mahbod, Ebrahim Bagheri, Wei Lu, and Ali A. Ghorbani. 2009. "A Detailed Analysis of the KDD CUP 99 Data Set." In *2009 IEEE Symposium on Computational Intelligence for Security and Defense Applications*, 1–6. https://doi.org/10.1109/CISDA.2009.5356528.

Tollefson, Rodika. 2020. "ICS/SCADA Malware Threats | Infosec." 2020. https://resources.infosecinstitute.com/topics/scada-ics-security/ics-scada-malware-threats/.

Townsend, Kevin. 2018. "Knowing Value of Data Assets Is Crucial to Cybersecurity Risk Management." SecurityWeek. December 3, 2018. https://www.securityweek.com/knowing-value-data-assets-crucial-cybersecurity-risk-management/.

Trend. 2012. "Spear-Phishing Email: Most Favored APT Attack Bait." https://documents.trendmicro.com/assets/wp/wp-spear-phishing-email-most-favored-apt-attack-bait.pdf.

Ussath, Martin, David Jaeger, Feng Cheng, and Christoph Meinel. 2016. "Advanced Persistent Threats: Behind the Scenes." *2016 Annual Conference on Information Science and Systems (CISS)*, March, 181–86. https://doi.org/10.1109/CISS.2016.7460498.

Villeneuve, Nart, and James Bennett. 2012. "Detecting APT Activity with Network Traffic Analysis." https://documents.trendmicro.com/assets/wp/wp-detecting-apt-activity-with-network-traffic-analysis.pdf.

Villeneuve, Nart, and James T. Bennett. 2014. "XtremeRAT: Nuisance or Threat?" Mandiant. 2014. https://www.mandiant.com/resources/blog/xtremerat-nuisance-or-threat.

Virvilis, Nikos, and Dimitris Gritzalis. 2013. "The Big Four - What We Did Wrong in Advanced Persistent Threat Detection?" In *2013 International Conference on Availability, Reliability and Security*, 248–54. https://doi.org/10.1109/ARES.2013.32.

Virvilis, Nikos, Dimitris Gritzalis, and Theodoros Apostolopoulos. 2013. "Trusted Computing vs. Advanced Persistent Threats: Can a Defender Win This Game?" In *2013 IEEE 10th International Conference on Ubiquitous Intelligence and Computing and 2013 IEEE 10th International Conference on Autonomic and Trusted Computing*, 396–403. https://doi.org/10.1109/UIC-ATC.2013.80.

Vukalovic, J., and Damir Delija. 2015. *Advanced Persistent Threats - Detection and Defense*. https://doi.org/10.1109/MIPRO.2015.7160480.

Wahla, Arfan, Lan Chen, Yali Wang, Rong Chen, and Fan Wu. 2019. "Automatic Wireless Signal Classification in Multimedia Internet of Things: An

Adaptive Boosting Enabled Approach." *IEEE Access* PP (November):1–1. https://doi.org/10.1109/ACCESS.2019.2950989.

Wang, Xiali, and Xiang Lu. 2020. "A Host-Based Anomaly Detection Framework Using XGBoost and LSTM for IoT Devices." *Wireless Communications and Mobile Computing* 2020 (October):1–13. https://doi.org/10.1155/2020/8838571.

Wang, Xu, Kangfeng Zheng, Xinxin Niu, Bin Wu, and Chunhua Wu. 2016. "Detection of Command and Control in Advanced Persistent Threat Based on Independent Access." In *2016 IEEE International Conference on Communications (ICC)*, 1–6. https://doi.org/10.1109/ICC.2016.7511197.

Wang, Yuan, Yongjun Wang, Jing Liu, and Zhijian Huang. 2014. "A Network Gene-Based Framework for Detecting Advanced Persistent Threats." In *2014 Ninth International Conference on P2P, Parallel, Grid, Cloud and Internet Computing*, 97–102. https://doi.org/10.1109/3PGCIC.2014.41.

Wang, Yuan, Yongjun Wang, Jing Liu, Zhijian Huang, and Peidai Xie. 2016. *A Survey of Game Theoretic Methods for Cyber Security.* https://doi.org/10.1109/DSC.2016.90.

Waqas, Muhammad, Kamlesh Kumar, Asif Ali Laghari, Umair Saeed, Muhammad Malook Rind, Aftab Ahmed Shaikh, Fahad Hussain, Athaul Rai, and Abdul Qayoom Qazi. 2022. "Botnet Attack Detection in Internet of Things Devices over Cloud Environment via Machine Learning." *Concurrency and Computation: Practice and Experience* 34 (4): e6662. https://doi.org/10.1002/cpe.6662.

Wright, John, Yi Ma, Julien Mairal, Guillermo Sapiro, Thomas S. Huang, and Shuicheng Yan. 2010. "Sparse Representation for Computer Vision and Pattern Recognition." *Proceedings of the IEEE* 98 (6): 1031–44. https://doi.org/10.1109/JPROC.2010.2044470.

Wu, Xindong, Vipin Kumar, J. Ross Quinlan, Joydeep Ghosh, Qiang Yang, Hiroshi Motoda, Geoffrey J. McLachlan, et al. 2008. "Top 10 Algorithms in Data Mining." *Knowledge and Information Systems* 14 (1): 1–37. https://doi.org/10.1007/s10115-007-0114-2.

Xu, Lei, Chunxiao Jiang, Jian Wang, Yong Ren, Jian Yuan, and Mohsen Guizani. 2015. "Game Theoretic Data Privacy Preservation: Equilibrium and Pricing." In *2015 IEEE International Conference on Communications (ICC)*, 7071–76. https://doi.org/10.1109/ICC.2015.7249454.

Yadav, Sandeep, Ashwath Kumar Krishna Reddy, A. L. Narasimha Reddy, and Supranamaya Ranjan. 2012. "Detecting Algorithmically Generated Domain-Flux Attacks With DNS Traffic Analysis." *IEEE/ACM Transactions on Networking* 20 (5): 1663–77. https://doi.org/10.1109/TNET.2012.2184552.

Yan, Xiaohuan, and J. Zhang. 2013. "A Early Detection of Cyber Security Threats Using Structured Behavior Modeling." In . https://www.semanticscholar.org/paper/A-Early-Detection-of-Cyber-Security-Threats-using-Yan-Zhang/92b0c21afbf1941cb27e707c50e51bd76a8b1d45.

Yang, Lu Xing, Pengdeng Li, Xiaofan Yang, and Yuan Yan Tang. 2017. "Security Evaluation of the Cyber Networks under Advanced Persistent Threats."

*IEEE Access* 5 (8053761): 20111–23. https://doi.org/10.1109/ACCESS.2017.2757944.

Yasar, Kinza, and Linda Rosencrance. 2021. "What Is an Advanced Persistent Threat (APT)? | Definition from TechTarget." Security. 2021. https://www.techtarget.com/searchsecurity/definition/advanced-persistent-threat-APT.

Zhang, Chongzhen, Yanli Chen, Yang Meng, Fangming Ruan, Runze Chen, Yidan Li, and Yaru Yang. 2021. "A Novel Framework Design of Network Intrusion Detection Based on Machine Learning Techniques." Edited by Savio Sciancalepore. *Security and Communication Networks* 2021 (January):1–15. https://doi.org/10.1155/2021/6610675.

Zhang, Ru, Yanyu Huo, Jianyi Liu, and Fangyu Weng. 2017. "Constructing APT Attack Scenarios Based on Intrusion Kill Chain and Fuzzy Clustering." *Security and Communication Networks* 2017 (December):e7536381. https://doi.org/10.1155/2017/7536381.

Zimba, Aaron, Hongsong Chen, Zhaoshun Wang, and Mumbi Chishimba. 2020. "Modeling and Detection of the Multi-Stages of Advanced Persistent Threats Attacks Based on Semi-Supervised Learning and Complex Networks Characteristics." *Future Generation Computer Systems* 106 (May):501–17. https://doi.org/10.1016/j.future.2020.01.032.

Zions Bancorporation. 2012. "A Case Study In Security Big Data Analysis." 2012. https://www.darkreading.com/cybersecurity-analytics/a-case-study-in-security-big-data-analysis.

Zou, Qingtian, Xiaoyan Sun, Peng Liu, and Anoop Singhal. 2020. "An Approach for Detection of Advanced Persistent Threat Attacks," no. 12 (December), 92–26. https://doi.org/10.1109/MC.2020.3021548.

www.ingramcontent.com/pod-product-compliance
Lightning Source LLC
LaVergne TN
LVHW051748050326
832903LV00029B/2789